The Rise and Fall of Little Voice

'Funny, sentimental, and savage by turns, bursting with compassion and life . . . Jim Cartwright is one of the mavericks of British theatre.' *Daily Telegraph*

'A Northern showbiz fairytale, a back-street Cinderella story, with a built-in kick.' *Guardian*

'Funny and abrasive . . . Cartwright brings a rich and steamy vocabulary to the stage.' *Observer*

Jim Cartwright lives in Lancashire, where he was born. His first play, *Road* (Royal Court, 1986), won the Samuel Beckett Award 1986, *Drama* magazine award 1986, was joint winner of the George Devine Award 1986 and *Plays and Players* Award 1986. The TV version won the Golden Nymph Award for the best film at the Monte Carlo Television Festival. His other plays include: *Bed* (Royal National Theatre, Cottesloe, 1989); *Two* (Bolton Octagon, 1989 and Young Vic, London, 1990), winner of the *Manchester Evening News* Best New Play Award in 1990; *The Rise and Fall of Little Voice* (Royal National Theatre and Aldwych Theatre, 1992), winner of the *Evening Standard* Best Comedy Award in 1992 and the 1993 Olivier Award for Best Comedy; *I Licked a Slag's Deodorant* (Royal Court at the Ambassadors Theatre, 1996).

Methuen Drama Modern Plays
First published in Great Britain in 1992
by Methuen Drama

ISBN 0 413 67130 5

A CIP catalogue record for this book
is available at the British Library

Typeset by Wilmaset Ltd, Wirral
Transferred to digital printing 2002

*The photograph on the cover is from the 1992 Royal National Theatre
production with Jane Horrocks as Little Voice (photo: © Mark Douet)*

Jim Cartwright

The Rise and Fall of Little Voice

METHUEN DRAMA

The Rise and Fall of Little Voice, produced by Michael Codron, was premièred in the Cottlesloe at the Royal National Theatre on 16 June 1992, with the following cast:

Mari Hoff	Alison Steadman
Little Voice (LV)	Jane Horrocks
Ray Say	Pete Postlethwaite
Sadie	Annette Badland
Billy	Adrian Hood
Phone Man	George Raistrick
Mr Boo	George Raistrick

Directed by Sam Mendes
Designed by William Dudley
Lighting by Mick Hughes
Music Terry Davies
Director of Movement Jane Gibson
Musicians Terry Davies (keyboards),
Michael Gregory (drums)

Stage Manager David Milling
Deputy Stage Manager Helen Bower
Assistant Stage Managers Andrew Eastcott
                                          Liz Ryder

Place: A Northern Town

Time: now

Set: A living room, kitchen attached, open plan. Up left, stairs to LV's bedroom. At side an alley and lamp-post are visible.

Act One

Darkness.

Darkness.

A long scream from **Mari**.

Mari There's one.

She screams again.

Mari There's another one. You scream.

LV No.

Mari No, you never scream, you hardly speak but you play your records, don't you?

LV You're drunk you.

In the blackness, we hear the sound of **Mari** *smashing things around.*

Mari And you put out the damn stinking lights, don't you?

Suddenly lights come up and **LV** *is at the fusebox on a chair. Record player in her room suddenly whirrs back into life, Shirley Bassey record very loud.*

Mari (*almost falling over*) Shut that up! Stop it! Get it off! Get it!

LV *runs upstairs fast. She gets in her room, takes it off. Begins putting another one on.*

Mari Come down.

LV *doesn't answer.*

Mari Okay, stay up. Play your old records. Bore me. Make me want to be sick all over the house.

Pause.

Mari Hey, hey, this better not cock up the putting in of my new phone tomorrow. It won't, will it?

LV No.

Mari Goodoh for that.

Mari *stands in living room tottering. Suddenly, record from* **LV***'s room really loud (Judy Garland, 'Come Rain or Come Shine'). She turns, feels sick, suddenly rushes to kitchen sink. Retching but nothing happening. She slides and knocks all the pans and plates off the side. Collapses on the kitchen floor.* **LV** *comes running downstairs. Music still playing loud. Helps* **Mari** *up. They stumble together.* **LV** *manages to get her back to the settee. They fall together on that.* **LV** *is trapped underneath her but manages to get out. She rolls her over on settee and tucks* **Mari***'s coat around her, takes off* **Mari***'s shoes, places them carefully. Covers* **Mari***'s ears with pillows. Starts to go upstairs.* **Mari** *moans and mumbles.* **LV** *stops, turns back, then carries on up.* **LV** *goes in her room. Turns the record player up even louder. Listens awhile. Bam. Electricity blows again.*

LV Not again.

Blackout.

Lights up. Living room. Morning.

A **Man** *and a very tall younger man (***Billy***) from the phone company are fitting in a phone. They have baggy overalls on.* **Mari** *in dressing gown. Smoking. Watching them.*

Mari Is it nearly in now?

Phone Man Nearly in.

Mari I'll be in touch with the world soon. I can't believe it, I'll be wired up to all parts.

Phone Man You will, love.

Mari Goodly. I spend my life and my fortune in them slot boxes, really I do.

The **Phone Man** *stands up.*

Mari Oh, them uniforms are not very becoming. You look like you've been thrown in a tool bag.

Phone Man *laughs.*

Mari It's put me right off that. And I always liked a man in uniform too.

Phone Man I bet you did.

Mari Eh, watch it Sparks, Sparkeler. Eh, speaking of sparks, you don't know nothing about electrickery do you? The wires of me home is crackling up on me.

Phone Man No, I'm just a phone chap.

Mari And a good un I hope. How we doing?

Phone Man Almost there.

Mari He's quiet in' he? (*Indicating tall one.*)

Phone Man He is.

Mari Is there anybody there? (*Laughs.*) Has he been disconnected? My daughter's like that.

Phone Man Speak to her, Bill.

Billy Hi.

Mari Eh, you're not the famous phone bill, are you?

They laugh.

Mari I'm on form this morning, bloody Nora. I'm excited you see. Hey, don't think I'm tight or anything not offering tea, but you see how I want the job done as quick as possible don't you. I want voices. And also I'm expecting a call, if you know what I mean.

Phone Man *laughs.*

Mari You do, don't you? Look at you though in that bag. You ought to complain. I might phone and complain for you. Good looking on the top, then that. Clark Gable in a bag, or should I say Clark Cable.

She laughs, then suddenly sings, excited.

'Oh, give me a phone where the phoneolohs phone.' Hurry up lads.

Phone Man *hands* **Billy** *a hammer.* **Billy** *turns to put it in toolbag.*

LV *enters from stairs.* **Billy** *drops hammer.* **LV** *jumps.*

Billy (*shy*) Sorry.

They both bend to pick it up. She picks it up first, gives it to him, half smiles.

Mari Oh, look at them two looking now. Hey, he doesn't speak as well. You could go out together and have a silent night, holy night.

LV *goes back upstairs.*

Mari Eh, what did I say? What did I say? And look at the red of him now, looky. Oh dear.

Suddenly music comes on loud again from upstairs.

Hang on, that's all you get when she's upset, crappaty records, full blast.

She hits the ceiling with something.

Cull it!

The music goes down.

Phone Man Right madam, it's done, I'll just ring
through to test the line.

Mari Oh, let me. Let me, go on.

Phone Man Okay.

He passes phone to her.

Mari Oh, this virgin blower and coil, this spanking
plastic, this phone of mine, Right, what's the number?

Phone Man 76543

Mari 7 . . . Oh, you press, I'll dialogue.

He does, she speaks.

Mari Hiyah love, we're on. Yes. Yes. PC Phone said I
could ring you. Put me down on the chart. Bye.

She puts the phone down. **Phone Man** *holds out a sheet and a pen.*

Phone Man Okay, could you sign this please. Er . . .?

She takes sheet.

Mari Mrs Hoff. Mari Hoff. (*As she takes pen.*) Crappaty
name in' it? My late husband, Frank, left it me. (*As she
signs.*) You can imagine my feelings on signing the
marriage register, Mr and Mrs F Hoff.

Phone Man Aye. (*Laughs.*)

She picks up the phone again.

Mari See you now.

Phone Man See you.

Mari (*dialling*) Thank you Clark Cable, byeoh.

They are leaving.

Billy (*quiet*) See you.

She ignores him. He takes a last glance upstairs, leaves. **Mari**
through on phone.

Mari Hello. Auntie Slit, is that you? It's Mari. I knew
you'd be up. You're doing the dogs, aren't you? Yes,
I'm just phoning to say, I'm phoneable now. Yeah I
have the phone, the phone. The line through. Yes. No.
No. I'm not going in work today . . . Not really ill shall
we say. No. NOT ILL, NO. (*To herself.*) Bloody hell.
Alright, I'm ill.

LV *enters down the stairs. Picks up newspaper. Heads for
kitchen.*

Mari No, our LV's looking after me. (*To* **LV**.) Aren't
you, love? Yes. She's fine. (*To* **LV**.) Come and have a
word with Auntie Slit! She won't. Oh, is that them
barking. Right you go Auntie, you go out and cut the
meats. Yes, bye now. Woof woof.

Puts phone down.

Deaf old clit. (*To* **LV**.) Make us a cuppa, love. Look
after me. Give us that paper. (**LV** *does.*) Oh take it
back, I don't like the front. What a thing to wake up to,
dying, lying and destruction.

She picks up phone again.

LV I hope you've paid for that.

Mari Oh shut up, it's me new toy and in fact me
lifeline. Okay? Live while you can, that's my motto and
your lesson (*Through on the phone.*) Hello, hiyah. Did I
wake you? Ooh get out of it. I bet you never slept last
night. I bet you. I do. I bet you. Just dinging to say
I've got one in, a phone you sex fiend, 61815. Burn it
between your breasts. Anyway, I'm going now. Got to
keep the line free. You know how it is when you're
expecting the call . . . Yes, he brought me home, he

sure did, but that's all you're getting till later. Phone in for the next thrilling instalment. Tell Mo and Licky but no one else. Bye, Marmainia. See see see ya. Leg over and out.

Puts phone down. **LV** *is sitting at kitchen table.*

Mari Shove us some food on something, LV. Go on, slap some food about for me, love. Come on.

LV There is none.

Mari Please don't tell me that.

Mari *gets up, goes to kitchen looking for food. She bangs her hand on kitchen table.*

Mari Oh, you're a misery you. Buck up will you.

LV *spills her drink.* **Mari** *returns to search.*

Mari What did you do last night?

LV *doesn't answer.*

Mari Play your records.
Play your records.
Bloody shit.

Mari *still searching for food.*

Mari You wanna live a bit.

LV Like you, you mean. The Merry Widow.

Mari Can't hear you. You'll have to speak up, Little Voice. That's all we ever said when you was a kid. (*Still looking for food.*) No bacon? I can't start the day without some dribbling fat. Can you? What you eating, a brown envelope?

LV A Ryvita.

Mari What, are you still a vegetarian?

LV *nods.*

Mari Oh yes. I forgot. (*Still looking for food.*) I'll tell you what, if there was a squealer in here, I'd chop it meself. Cut, cut.

She leaves kitchen, comes back into the living room.

Mari What's on the telly? (*Turns it on, turns it off before it even comes on.*) Oh sod that. Oh sod this, I'm going down the caf'. But first, ring, phone, ring. Give us paper while I'm waiting.

LV *passes it to her.*

Mari (*looks at her*) Why are you so miserable?

LV *ignores her.*

Mari Hey and listen you. I've been meaning to have a word with you for sometime about something. You never speak, right, you never leave the house. I want to know once and for all, are you agraphobical? Because if you are, you can get out.

LV I'm not.

Mari Right then. (*Reads on.*)

Mari *sits on sofa.*

Mari Come on cock, please brew.

LV *ignores her.*
Mari *throws newspaper up.*

Mari Bloody hell. Bloody hell, eh?

Knock at door.

Mari Come in, Sadie.

A great big fat woman comes in. The neighbour.

Mari Sit down. Crush a chair anywhere you like.

Sadie Okay.

Mari Do you want a cuppa or 'owt?

Sadie Okay.

Mari Make us one while you're at it.

Sadie Okay.

Mari Where am I this morning, the Okay Corral or what? Frig me. Don't put loads of bloody sugar in yours an all. You emptied half the bloody bag yesterday. (*Looks at the page of newspaper still left in her lap.*) Frig me up and down, look what's happened in the news.

Sadie What?

Mari She's named him and he didn't know.

She throws it away.

Do you like me phone?

Sadie (*looking*) Okay that.

Mari Okay! Wait 'til it starts trilling. In fact we shouldn't have long to wait as I'm expecting a call this morning.

Sadie (*excited*) A chap?

Mari On the nail, Sade.

LV *stands to leave.*

Mari Where you going?

LV *just makes her way upstairs.*

Mari Don't start that bloody music again. I've no head for that. (*To* **Sadie**.) Can you hear it next door?

Sadie At times, when I'm pegging out.

Mari (*to* **LV**) Did you hear that. (*To* **Sadie**.) Bloody crazed chil' she is. I'm sure it's that player what's sucking up all my 'tricity and causing sparks. Go on off upstairs like an ignorant. She bugs me at times. Though I'm all she's got and she's all I've got, besides me arse and tits. Where's that brew.

LV *puts a record on. It plays.* **Mari** *throws something at ceiling beneath* **LV**'s *room.*

Mari Cull it!

LV *turns it down. She gently puts her head on the player.*

Mari I don't know what to do with her. She's morbidity itself, just plays them damn records her Dad left her, over and a over. Just them, nothing else, on and on. That's not health is it, Sade? But what can I do? You can only do so much, can't you Sade?

Sadie *brings really steaming tea over.*

Sadie You can. You said chap?

Mari Oh yes . . . yes. (*Takes tea*.) Tar. Let me see yours. (**Sadie** *shows*.) I can see the sugar! Will you stop that.

Sadie Okay.

Mari Go on, drink it now.

They both sip.

Mari Well, Sadie, what a night! What-a-night! What a championship neet! In fact come here and belt me. Calm me down with a smack sandwich so I can tell the tale. Belt me.

Sadie *comes over and hits* **Mari**'s *two cheeks simultaneously.*

Mari Tar. Well, I copped off again with that Ray. I did it again. He had no choice. You couldn't have got a bar between us last night, I became his side. I was eye to eye with him all night. There was virtually only enough virtual room to move our drinks table to gob. The turn was a romantic singer, thank frig, and the music was in our heads, in our heads and in his wandering hands. Everyone's coming up to Ray allt' time, 'Howdo', 'Alright'. He knows so many people and I'm on his arm and his hands on my arse as he speaks to them. My arse. My golden old arse in Ray Say's hands. You can see how I am there. A queen. Queen for the night. He motored me home about a million miles an hour. I don't know what kinda car it is. One o'them big ones that bloody go, pistols in the back, all that, toaster in the dashboard, lights blinking on and off, put me up, put me down, put me up, put me down seats, thick as beds. Crack oh round the bloody roads we was. Heart in mouth, hand on leg, the lot. Then screeching to a halt outside, did you not hear us? You must be dead if you didn't. I saw every other curtain in the bitching road twitch. Then he comes at me with this pronto snog, lip-lapping like hell. That's men for you in it Sade, if you can remember. Lip-a-lapping, like old hell he was. But at least he's a lot better than most, at least he knows how to slide and dart and take a throat. At least there's always the thick wad of his wallet up against your tit for comfort.

Sadie Aye.

Mari *picks up a piece of newspaper.*

Mari Have you seen the headlines on the paper, look. Slavering, slavering. Men are always slavering. Only joking. You can't read, can you Sade?

Sadie I can get by, if the print's of a size.

Mari I know what you mean. You were a dab hand on the betting slips though, weren't you? When you had your trouble though, weren't you? In fact, he works on the tracks, Ray.

Sadie Is he a bookie?

Mari Sure. Besides having a finger in a load of other pies. Some too scorching bloody burning hot for his own good if you get my mean. In fact, he's moving into artist's management at the moment, you know. Yes. He's got Trigger Smit and Elaine, The Trumpet 4, Flaggy the Cot Poodle, and a couple of strippers at the moment. But he'll make it, he'll make it in anything, Ray Say. He's one o'them, give him an inch, he'll take the coal shed, how can I say, a lovable twat sort of type. (*Sips.*) See, partly partly, no, mainly mainly, that's why I got the (*Indicating phone.*) ragbone in. I've got to be on call. It's got to be smooth for him going out with me. I must win him. I've got to keep him. He's got a lot of young bitches into him a quart my age. I know they haven't got my wizzle and mince but I'm taking no chances Sade, how can I at my time of strife?

Music comes on loud again.

Mari Oh trash that calypso!

It goes down again.

Mari I've got to eat though or I won't be able to hold my own with him down the blower. Must be quick though, I'll phone and warn them. (*Rings cafe off a card she has, gets through.*) Caf-Caf, are you open? Right I'm coming down. In me slippers. I want Crackerbarrell on toast and a fuck hot tea. Tar. (*Puts phone down.*)

Sadie *gets up to leave.*

Mari While you're at the door get me me coat.

Sadie *does and holds it for her,* **Mari** *slips it on.* **Sadie** *goes out.* **Mari** *shouts upstairs.*

Mari I'm going down the caf'. If anyone phones before I return, this is more important than your life girl, tell them I'll be back in five minutes. Tell them that and that's all, alright? ALRIGHT? Are you receiving me?

LV *(from bedroom)* Yes.

Mari Toodle pip.

She leaves. The music is turned up full, ('I who have nothing', Shirley Bassey). **LV** *emerges from bedroom, comes downstairs. Music playing loud. She goes in kitchen. She opens fridge door, looks in.*

LV Oh God.

Closes it. Fills and plugs kettle in. Goes and picks pieces of newspaper up, tidies a little. Phone rings. She looks at it, scared. Looks at it. Lowers her hand over it. Retreats. Runs upstairs, turns off record player. Peeps down, it's still ringing. Comes down, frightened. Suddenly, a knock at the door. She looks at door. Knock again. She opens it. It is the shy phone boy, **Billy**.

Billy *(shy)* Hello, I put your phone in.

She nods.

Billy I think we left our hammer.

She looks, sees it, nods. Steps back to let him in.

Billy Oh.

He goes to get it. It's by the phone. He gets it.

Billy Your phone's ringing.

She nods. Looks at it. He can see she's uncomfortable.

Billy Do you want me to get it for you?

She nods. He picks it up.

Billy Er . . . Mari . . . Er . . .

LV She's gone Caf-Caf.

Billy What?

LV Back soon.

Billy She will be back soon. Right. Right.

Puts phone down.

Ray, he'll ring back.

LV Thanks.

Billy (*clutching hammer*) Yes. (*Not knowing what to say.*) I don't like talking on phones an' all. An' I work with 'em.

She nods. They look at each other. He wants to say more, but can't.

Billy See you then.

He goes to leave. Stops.

Billy See you.

LV *nods. He leaves. She closes door. Kettle explodes.*

Blackout.

Lights up.

Living room, night. **LV** *is sitting in dark. TV on, light flickering up her face, an old Judy Garland film.*

Door suddenly bursts open.

Mari *there. Switches light on.*

Mari Right you. You've got a fucking second to get in shape.

Runs from back, leaps over the settee. Turns TV off. Goes back round towards door.

Mari Perk girl perk. (*At door.*) Aye come in Ray. Come in. Here he is (*She holds her hand towards door.*) Mr Ray Say.

Man comes in, forties, in a suit, hair quiffed slightly.

Mari Here it is, my home. My phone. My kitchen. My wall. My telly. My daughter.

Ray How do.

Mari Ray. Sun Ray. Sting Ray. Ray Gun. My Ray of hope. I'm a frigging just inta him so. (*She kisses him. To* **LV**.) Well, say hello at least. You miserable spot. I've warned you.

LV (*awkward, almost inaudible*) Hello.

Mari Oh, she's a miserable misery. What you having Raymondo and don't say nowt rude, ha!

Ray What's in?

Mari Everything your throat could desire.

She suddenly speeds round house collecting half empty bottles and standing them in the middle of the room. One from under a table. One from behind a cushion. One from the washing machine. One from under the telly. At one point she makes **LV** *stand up while she looks under the settee for a bottle, it rolls out. She assembles them all in the middle of the floor.*

Mari There.

Ray I'll have a cup of tea, tar.

Mari You'll what? (*Laughing.*) He'll have a cup o'tea. Har. Ha ha he. (*Looks at* **LV**.) Look, look, she nearly laughed then, din't you eh? Nearly.

LV *stands up and heads for her bedroom.*

Mari Hey, don't just go like that, you rude slit. Hey!

Ray Leave her, she's alright.

Mari No. It's not right, she spoils everything, her. I'm trying to make an impression and she can't even be swivel to a friend. The little tiny slit!

She kicks a chair over, boots the bottles.

Mari Oh what am I doing and in front of you! Oh well, that's it, I give up. This is my crappaty home, and this is how I am Ray, no gracey airs, and if you don't like it piss off out of it.

Ray Hey, hey, calm down. Don't get mad at me. I didn't say anything about anything.

Mari Oh okay, come on, let's roll about.

She pulls him on settee. His drink goes flying. They snog and roll about.

Suddenly, from above, the sound of Judy Garland loud, 'The man that got away.

Ray What's that?

Mari I'll shut her up.

Ray Leave it.

Mari *hits ceiling again.*

Mari Cull it!

The music doesn't go down. Angry. She starts to go upstairs.

Mari Right!

Ray Hey, hey, never mind. Come on. Come here.

Mari (*stops*) Ha. You're right. Sod the bitch. We'll have our own on.

She goes to radiogram, puts her own record on. Turns it up. Both are going now. She goes back to **Ray**. *They roll about snogging. Suddenly the lights go. The electrics have gone again.* **Ray** *stops. The two record players grind to a halt.*

Mari You've blown me fuse.

They laugh and carry on. **LV** *begins singing 'The man that got away' from where the record left off. It sounds just like the record. The song continues for some time.* **Ray** *and* **Mari** *snogging. Then suddenly* **Ray** *stops.*

Ray How can that be, has she a radio?

Mari That's not 'her', that's her.

Ray What?

Mari I mean, that's not the record, that's LV.

Ray No.

Mari Yeah.

Ray No.

Mari Yeah.

Ray No.

Mari Fucking hell.

Ray That's her singing, but that's amazing.

Mari Amazin' Ray sin. Come on, let's roll about.

Ray Hold on. How can she do that?

Mari I don't know, throat twisting, I presume. Roll.

Ray I still don't believe it.

Mari Look, Ray, she plays 'em all the time, every God sented sec'. They're stuck in her head. She can sing them. It gets on my wick. End of story. Come on. I'm ready.

Ray Where did she get them?

Mari When he died, he left them her.

Ray Your husband?

Mari Yeah, Frank.

Ray What was he like then?

Mari Put it this way, he listened to women's records.

Ray So.

Mari Put it this way. He was thin and tall and hardly spoke. When I was a teenager, I thought I'd found Gary Cooper but ended up I'd found Olive Oil. He was a length of dry stick that bored me bra-less. He sat folded up in that chair there resembling misery in its many fucking forms and he tried to make me the same. He could not succeed. Come on lover boy.

Ray (*still towards the singing*) Hang on, I'm listening.

Mari Come on, lover boy, I'm contorted here.

Ray Ssssh. Hold on.

Mari Oh, I'm off then.

She closes her eyes and immediately falls asleep. **Ray** *listens intently till the song ends. Then he starts clapping.*

LV, *upstairs, afraid.*

Blackout.

Living room/kitchen. Morning

LV *comes downstairs, goes in kitchen. Opens bread bin. Takes out a curled crust of white bread from the bottom of it. She is heading for toaster with it.* **Ray** *appears from stairs, pulling on* **Mari**'s *dressing gown over bare chest and trousers.*

Ray Hi.

She drops the precious piece of bread.

Ray Don't get a shock, it's only me, Ray Say, remember.

She doesn't speak, goes to plug in kettle. It flashes. She jumps again.

Ray You wanna watch that. Could fetch the house down. And so could you with what you did last night.

LV *retreats further into kitchen, bit afraid. Gets a glass of water.*

Ray Bloody marvellous that. Who else do you do, eh?

She starts to go.

Ray Don't go. I'm interested cause I'm showbusiness meself you see. R Say very personal management. Your mam must have told you. No? Well never mind. (*Indicating bread.*) Shame about the crust cock, here let me rustle you up one of Ray Say's famous breakfassays. I do 'em all the time for my artistes, when we's on a foreign engagement. Not all glamour our game you know.

He opens fridge.

Oh God.

Closes it quick.

Ray You ever bin to Spain?

LV No.

Ray Last weekend I flew a couple of the girls and myself out to do a show. I know an old jockey runs a bartello there, 'The Prince Charles', good gig, good gig. Bloody mad out there though. Raging, love, wild. Not like the postcards. I've got two scars somewhere I brought back for souvenirs. One on me chest, see. And one on me lip, look. (*He gets close, she looks.*) Can I just say again while you're this close. Bloody marvellous what you did last night. Marvellous in the dark there, something I'll never forget. Do you mind if I ask you something love?

LV *shakes her head.*

Ray How the hell on earth do you do it?

LV Uh, I . . .

Ray No, no, don't try. Don't. You wouldn't know. The true performer never does, take it from me. I understand the artiste, you see. Do you know Wild Trigger Smit and his good lady Elaine. I'm the only one in showbiz who can handle him. She thinks the sun shines out of me, Elaine, especially now I've got him off the knives and back on vocals. He were on 'Opportunity Knocks' in '69, you know. They say he would a won but he butted the make-up man or summat. He's not like that now though old Trig'. (*As he turns to shelves.*) Thank frig.

He casually pulls a packet of cornflakes down, looks in.

Ray What's this, a box of privet leaves, urgh they's all green.

He puts them back.

Ray I'll tell you what, what say you and me continue our conversation down the Caf-Caf.

LV No thanks.

Ray (*surprised*) No . . . I'll pay and everything.

Gets his fat wallet out.

LV No.

Ray Okay, suit yourself.

LV But.

Ray Yeah.

LV Er . . .?

Ray Hey fire away love.

LV In showbusiness, did you ever meet Shirley Bassey?

Ray Now then . . . Shirley, to be honest no love, our paths have never crossed. I've met Monkhouse though. (*Sees she's not impressed.*) And of course Cilla.

LV Cilla?

Ray Yeah.

LV No.

Ray Sure.

LV (*eager*) What's she like?

Ray Alreet.

LV I've got one of hers upstairs.

Ray You can't do her an' all can you?

He starts putting his wallet away. While he's distracted and not looking, she speaks in a Cilla-type voice.

LV Hello, do you know who this is Ray?

Ray *turns white.*

Ray (*seriously shocked*) Christ, I can't believe that. Take it from me. Hey . . . Hey. Honest love. Take it from me . . . Does no one know about this?

LV No. (*Shakes her head.*)

Ray I can't believe it. What does your Mam say?

LV Nowt.

Ray Nowt?

LV No.

Ray Listen seriously LV. Listen, you are my discovery. I've found you right, me, always remember that. In fact here, have one o'me new cards. (*He gets one out.*) Gold, look.

She is fascinated by the glint of it, but won't take it.

Ray No, here you are, you're the first to have one a these.

She almost takes it, but doesn't.

Ray No, there love. I wouldn't give one a these to everyone.

She takes it.

Ray Now listen LV. I know you're quiet, your Mam's told me that, but together you and me we could set the place on fire.

LV You're a nutter you.

She goes.

Ray And you're a star.

She goes upstairs.

Ray, *excited, runs to phone. Dials.*

Ray Hello! Hello, is Mr Boo in, I need to speak to him now . . . It's Ray Say, Say, Say, yeah. No, it can't wait, no. Hold him there. I'm coming down now!

He puts phone down, starts off upstairs to finish dressing. Half way up he meets **Mari** *coming down, looking crap.*

Ray Marrii!

Mari Don't speak to me. Don't speak for a minute.

Ray *laughs and continues upstairs.*

Mari *comes down. She goes in kitchen area hunting for an aspirin. She finds one. Then can't find a cup in all the mess on the draining board.*

Mari Cup cup.

Knocks something off draining board.

Mari Aarrrgh!

Drops aspirin into an empty milk bottle. Puts water in. While it's dissolving, she holds her head at the sound it's making. Drinks it.

Ray *reappears, bounding downstairs, putting on tie. Jacket over arm.*

Mari Darling, how are you?

Goes to embrace him. **Ray** *is dressing as he speaks.*

Ray I've got to dash Mari. But what can I say? It's happened at last, eh! I'm so excited, it's like at the races when you've found yourself a little nag no one's noticed but you know you're onto a certainty and you're feeling, this is it! She is the one. Do you know what I mean?

A knock on the door.

Mari Go on, yes! Yes! I'm with you lad. Yes . . .

Ray It's like . . .

Mari Yeah. Yeah. (*Desperate.*) Ignore that.

It's too late, **Ray** *is opening it. It's* **Billy**.

Billy It's, er, me again. Er, just come to see if your phone's still alright.

Mari *snatches handset up. Holds it out to him.*

Mari Is that its sound?

Billy Yes.

Mari It's reet!

Slams door.

Mari On Ray, on.

Ray (*forgetting where he was*) Er . . .

Mari You were under starters orders and you were off!

Ray Yeah. It's not just my future, it's yours.

Mari Oh my God.

Ray I still can't believe it. It's what I've been looking for for ages. And here it is under this roof, under me very nose. All I can say is . . .

Knock on door. **Rays** *opens it.*

Mari No, leave it! For Godsake leave it!

Sadie *is standing there.*

Ray (*as he leaves*) I'll be back soon. I can't leave it. Not this. Best to act fast when you're this sure eh?

Mari *nods frantically.*

Ray It's just one o'them once in a lifetime things.

He passes **Sadie** *and leaves.* **Mari** *takes her by the sleeve and silently draws her in the house.*

Mari Sadie, did you hear that utterance? Did you? Did you hear what Say sayeth. It were almost on the tip there of his raspberry tongue, he wants me. I can't believe it Sade. The bastard wants me. Get Jackson 5 on, Sadie. We always play it when we've something to celebrate, don't we?

Sadie, *happy, runs to radiogram and gets it on.*

Mari At last. At last. Saved, secured. I shall go to the ball. Oh darlings from the sky.

The music comes on: 'I want you back' Jackson 5. They dance all around the room. Music blaring. They dance till they have to stop.

Mari Oh, oh stop. I can't breathe.

Sadie *turns it off. They collapse on settee and chairs.*

Mari Din't I say to you though Sadie, when I first spied him, I knew there was summat down for us. I just had that twat-bone feeling, and you know me, I can predict rain with that.

She suddenly gets up.

Hey, I'd better get dressed up, who knows when he will return. Where's me knickers and bra?

Pulls some out the washing basket, they are all tangled up with a line of other bras and knickers and suspender belts and tea towels etc. She can't separate them.

(*Speaking as she tries.*) I'm one high razzamatazza in here today. (*Hitting her chest.*) It's like there's a circus parade passing over my paps. What a life, life can be.

In the end she just takes them all up in a long trail. She heads for the stairs trailing them all behind her.

(*As she ascends.*) Sadie, make yourself a cup of sugar with some tea in it. I shall be down shortly.

She goes upstairs and into her room, slams door. **Sadie**, *still panting, goes into kitchen to make tea.*

LV *alone in her room. Suddenly, we see a yellow 'Cherry Picker' (platform on a winch, used by telephone engineers and for lighting maintenance on lamp-posts etc.) coming high round the side of house.* **Billy** *is in it, holding a hammer.*

It comes along alley and up level with her window. **LV** *screams.* **Billy** *speaks.*

Billy Just seeing if wires are alright.

She looks at him amazed. Can't hear him through the window.

Billy (*louder*) Just seeing if wires are alright!

She opens window.

Billy Just seeing! . . .

Nearly knocks her over with shout, quickly quietens.

Billy . . . if wires are alright.

Starts whistling. Whistling as he looks at wall, up and down.

Billy Do you go out much?

LV No.

Billy *whistling.*

Billy Are you a telly fan?

LV No.

Billy *whistling. Presses button, goes out to side a bit, away from her view.*

Billy Are you going anywhere for your holidays?

LV No.

Whistling trails off.

Billy There are no wires.

LV Eh?

Billy I should be up a telegraph pole three streets away, but I come here.

Presses button, returns to window.
They look at each other.

Billy I don't know what to say now.

Pause. They look at each other.

Billy I'm like this at work. Then when I do speak they all jump like I've dropped a brick in a bucket.

He smiles nervously. She does a bit.

Billy I'm Billy. Can I ask you your name.

LV LV.

Billy Oh, does that stand for something?

LV Little Voice.

Billy Oh, cause of your soft voice.

LV I think it's more cause no one could never hear me.

Billy I can.

Pause.

Billy Your Mam's a live wire in't she. Bloody hell.

LV Aye.

Billy I live with me Grandad. It's quiet in our house, the clock an all that.

LV Ours is a mad house.

Billy Aye. (*Pause.*) Hope you don't mind having a chat this high up.

LV No, do you?

Billy No. No. Safe as houses these. It goes higher than this, this. See.

He presses a button. Machine rises to above the roof height.

Billy I like going up. Better view.

LV What view?

Billy (*looking*) Backs. Backs. Works. Works. Backs. Works. Backs. And the last chimney.

LV I can't even see that.

Billy No, your view's blocked by Vantona.

LV Me Mam works there.

Billy Oh aye. Maybe I can see her through one of the little windows.

LV You won't. She hardly ever goes in.

Billy Oh.

He presses button, comes down. **LV** *stands up. They face each other.*

Billy Little Voice, I don't know what's come over me. I've not been able to rest till I could come here again.

I've only been like this once before. That's when I first
saw Blackpool illuminations.

Pause.

Billy Do *you* by any chance, like, by any chance, light
displays at all, LV? I only ask 'cause it's the one thing I
can really talk about and I don't want to dry up on
you, not now.

She smiles, confused. He takes this as permission to continue.

I've got me Grandad's shed on the allotment and I've
blacked out the windows. I . . . No, I'll say no more, it
can be boring to the non-enthusiast.

LV No, you're alright.

Billy You sure.

LV *nods.*

Inside that shed. Inside that shed. When I throw the
switch, Little Voice, you wun't believe it. Light. Up the
walls. Off the ceiling, caught light, bent light, beams
under beams of it, colours, colours coming up through
colours you've never seen. Shades to make you happy,
shades to make you sad, shades to make you Voom!

The last word he sent out so powerfully in his exitement **LV**
falls back in surprise.

~~Sorry!~~

LV No.

Billy So sorry.

LV It's alright.

Billy I don't know what it is, after the illuminations,
that was it. I'd only play with torches and Christmas

tree lights, I spent all me youth with the curtains closed, fascinated, helpless as a moth.

Pause.

Only thing is I'll never show. ~~Me Grandad says I'm like an artist painting masterpieces and keeping them under the stairs,~~ he keeps mythering me to do the lights for his pensioners' 'do' down the working man's club. I always say no. Somehow though, I don't know. After talking to you, telling you. Maybe I shall do it. I don't know. If I did would you come down?

LV I don't know. I don't go out.

Billy Would you think about it. I could go and find out all the details. I really would be honoured. I really would be so . . . If you could just see them, LV. (*Almost to himself.*) ~~I'd take from above, I'd bring down some heaven. Poor old sods they'd think they were getting a mirror ball and a couple of spotlights and they'd be flying when I'd done.~~

Mari *comes out of her bedroom, stops on landing.*

Mari What's going on. You talking to yourself now gal!

LV (*to* **Billy**) Sorry. I got go.

She hurriedly closes window.

Mari Is that you and your voices.

Billy LV, the lights.

LV *is gone inside. He presses button, begins to disappear back round corner.*

Mari (*to herself*) Crazed.

Mari *comes grandly downstairs, tarted up.* **Sadie** *is in living room.*

Well, Sadie, how do I look? And don't say okay or I'll poke your Pilsbury dough.

Sadie *has a mouthful of something, so just nods approvingly.*

What you eating? I thought there was nothing in.

Sadie Cornflakes.

Mari Oh.

Suddenly, the sound of a car outside screeching up. **Mari** *looks out of window.*

Mari It's Ray Say. I didn't expect him so soon.

She rushes to mirror; lacquer can and sherry bottle at side. Starts lacquering and quick drinking in turn.

Mari Lacquer! Liquor! Lacquer! Liquor!

She lacquers all over her hair and everywhere fast.

Mari Oh I've had the colour shocked out of me.

Slaps both her cheeks hard.

Mari Come on up you young apples. You cheeky cheeks.

She looks out again.

Mari He's got someone wi' him. Maybe it's the vicar.

Sadie *stands up.*

Mari Don't take me serious, Sade. (*To herself.*) Fat sucker.

Sadie *sits again.*

Mari No, no, it's that bloke from the club, what the hell's he doing with him? Come on, Sadie, sod off. I need some seats free. (*Changing her mind.*) No, no stay and get drinks.

Knock at door. **Mari** *opens it.* **Ray** *and* **Mr Boo** *step in.*

Mari Darling, din' expect you back so swoon.

Ray Mari, you know Mr Boo from down the club.

Mr Boo Call me Lou.

Billy (*almost curtsying*) Pleasured I'm sure, Mr Lou.

Ray No, Lou's his first name.

Mari (*almost curtsying again*) Sorry. Sit down.

Ray This is Little Voice's mother.

Mari (*to* **Ray**) Hang on. Little Voice? What's going on?

Ray Like I said Mari, LV's a real discovery, a once in a lifetime thing. That's why I've dragged Mr Boo straight down here to hear her.

Mr Boo *nods.*

Mari LV?

Ray Yeah.

She goes away to her liquor bottle by mirror.

Ray Will you just get her down for us, cock, Mr Boo's not got long you see, have you?

Mr Boo (*looking at watch*) Nope.

Mari (*drinking*) You know where she rots. Fetch her yourself.

Ray (*goes upstairs a little. Softly*) LV! LV! It's Ray Say, remember? Can you come down love. I've brought someone to hear you do your stuff love?

Mr Boo *coughs.*

Ray Someone important LV love!

No response. He goes right up to **Mari.**

Ray Mari, will you go and get her?

Mari (*snaps at Ray*) You're tapped, you. She'll not sing in public, LV.

Ray Hey, I want Boo to hear her sing, alright?

Mari She'll not throat on cue, LV.

Mr Boo Everything alright, Say?

Ray Oh aye.

Mr Boo Just reminding you lad, I've not all day.

Ray Aye. (*To* **Mari.**) Listen, my reputation's at stake here, get up them dancers and get her down.

Mari Easier said than done.

Ray Listen Mari, I want her down. What's up with you?

Mari You.

Ray Eh?

Mari You with your 'special' and all that, the 'one and only' and all that. I thought you meant me din't I?

Ray (*struggling now*) Hey. I do. Bloody hell, Mari, I did. I do. Yes. You are special, bloody hell, you know that. I meant I found you both at the same time. That's what I meant. Eh? Course I did.

Puts his arm around her.

Ray Eh?

Mari Oooh you.

Mari *goes up close to* **Ray**, *almost kissing.*

Mari Elvis breath.

Ray Go on, get her down love.

Mari Well, anything for you love, but I think you've backed your first loser there Ray, sorry to say.

She goes to stairs. Stops on first step, looks over to **Sadie** *and* **Mr Boo**. **Mr Boo** *reading newspaper.* **Sadie** *staring out.*

Mari Sadie talk to Lou Boo.

Carries on upstairs to **LV**'s *room.*

Sadie Okay. (*To* **Mr Boo**.) Hello.

Mr Boo Hi.

Sadie *just turns back to looking out.* **Mr Boo** *glares over at* **Ray**.

Ray (*to* **Mr Boo**) Won't be a minute now Mr Boo.

Mr Boo *cracks out the paper and reads again.*

Mari LV. LV.

LV *is inside, album covers all around her and up in front of her face as she reads the back of one.* **Mari** *goes in.*

Mari Come down, Ray wants you a minute.

She doesn't reply.

Mari Ray wants you for a minesota, will you get down?

LV What for?

Mari You know what for, you've got him thinking you can do summat or summat. He wants you down anyway, show some showman or summat.

LV It's private.

Mari Private, my privates. You're just damn selfish and useless and can do nowt but whisper and whine like your Father before you, a couple of nowts.

LV *turns away, behind record sleeve.*

A load of dirty auld discs and a clapped out player. The sum of your Father's life. Just a load of old rubbish nobody wants.

LV *covers her ears.* **Mari** *snatches LP cover from her.* **LV** *gets it back.*

LV Don't dare ever touch these.

Mari Up yours, stick leg.

She goes out and downstairs to **Ray**.

Mari (*on her way down*) She won't come down.

Ray What?

Mari Just as I told you, she won't sing, told you.

Mr Boo What's happening, Say?

Ray She's not quite prepared yet, Mr Boo, late sleeper and all that, see.

Mr Boo Well I've gotta be off. Sorry and all that, Say. Maybe some other time, eh.

Ray Hold on.

Mr Boo (*to* **Sadie**) Goodbye er . . .

Sadie Sadie May.

Mr Boo Sadie May, nice to make your acquaintance. Bye all.

Starts to leave. **Ray** *goes after him.*

Ray Mr Boo wait. I'm sure we can persuade her. Hold on, give me a minute. I'll get her down. Believe me Boo! It's like I said.

Mr Boo*'s out.* **Ray***'s out after him.* **Mari** *follows on.* **Sadie** *after. Door slams.*

Mr Boo Hard to tell when I've heard nowt.

Mari Leave it Ray.

Ray (*to* **Mr Boo**) Come back inside.

Mr Boo Enough's enough. I've got to get back down the club.

Ray Look, you know me. I wouldn't fetch you down here for nowt. You've got to hear her. I can sort it, you know me.

LV *upstairs has heard the door slam. She sits on her bed, sings to herself. 'Never Never' (Shirley Bassey). Suddenly voices outside subside to silence.*

Ray *appears from corner of building listening and stands under lamp-post.*

Mr Boo *comes next and joins him. Then* **Mari** *and last* **Sadie**. *They cluster under the lamp, almost like carol singers, listening. She sings a couple of verses. Stops.*

Ray That was her.

Mr Boo Wasn't.

Ray Was.

Mr Boo Wasn't.

Ray Was.

Mr Boo No.

Ray Yes.

Mari (*to herself*) Here we fucking go again.

LV *starts to sing again. Changes song to 'Somewhere over the Rainbow' (Judy Garland) sings some, then hums softly.*

Ray That was her an all.

Mr Boo Well, it's remarkable that. You have a remarkable daughter there, Mrs Hoff.

Mari Thank you, I'm sure.

Mr Boo Well, Ray, we must have her if you can arrange it. There's the makings of a class act there, class. We could do a lot with that.

Ray It'll cost you.

Mr Boo I expected it to.

Ray Come on, Mr Boo.

They start to leave.

Ray (*to* **Mari**) We're off to talk fine details and finances.

Mari (*following*) I'm with you. Don't forget me. The flesh and blood management.

LV *picks up song again.* **Sadie** *left standing alone below lamp, cheek on hands, rapt.* **LV** *finishes song, totally unaware of what's taking place.*

Blackout.

Night. Living room.

Mari *and* **Ray** *come in, drunk.* **Ray**'s *tie down. They sit on settee.*

Mari Roll about. Roll about.

They do. She flings her arms about.

Mari Roll about me.

They continue.

Mari Eh, eh. I'm going to get the little star up and tell her the news. Where am I?

She stands.

Mari Shove me in the right direction.

Ray Arrgh, leave it to the morning.

Mari No no. It might change her little life, this. Might bloody change mine for once. I never thought anyone would want to see her. Never in a million.

Ray Sometimes what's under your nose, you don't smell. It's the way of it.

Mari I know, I know. You have a wisdom, Ray. Also, you know what to say in many situations, also you know how to have a laugh, dress and drive. Also you

have a fair sized dong. I'm glad I made your
acquaintance.

Ray I'm going for a slash.

Tottering to stairs, she goes up. **Ray** *follows her and goes in
toilet. She taps on* **LV**'*s door, goes in.* **LV** *is asleep.* **Mari**
*looks at her, stumbles, reaches to wake her, then stops. Stumbles,
sits on bedside. Reaching out again but gently strokes her hair.
Tucks her in. Suddenly* **Ray** *bursts in through door.*

Ray Alright! Well then! What does she think eh?

Mari *stumbles, falls off bed.* **LV** *wakes.*

LV Arrgh, what's . . . Aarrgh.

Mari Love, lovey, don't worry. It's me, me and Ray.

Ray Hiyah.

LV What do you want? What you doing?

Mari We've got some good news for you.

Ray Stupendous news actually like.

Mari Mr Boo, he's a man would like you to sing at the
club, yes, on the stage.

Ray Sing what you like.

LV (*dumbstruck*) No, no.

Mari No, listen love. He'll pay. Yes, he will pay. Good
money an all. Could be up to £50. Right Ray?

Ray Right and that's only the start of it.

LV No.

Mari Ray'll look after you, he knows all about it. And all you'll have to do is sing. Sing, what you like best doing anyways. Sing.

LV No, please.

Mari You might feel shy. I know what you're thinking.

Ray You might be shy at first.

Mari Natural that.

Ray I had a girl recently wouldn't say boo to a goose, now she's topping the bill at the Reform Club.

Mari Is that the stripper?

Ray Well, yes, but it's similar, int'it. Similar case, Tina.

LV Please go. Please. Please.

She pulls covers up around her, backs into corner like she's being hunted.

LV Please go. Please.

They go. Close door behind them and head downstairs.

Ray Bloody hell, I din' think she'd take it quite like that.

Mari Aye. Give her a while to let it sink in. Actually I'll go up, go up and have another word with her.

Ray (*takes hold of her*) No, no, you were right, leave it.

Mari What a hold you have on you, Ray, firm but fancy. Let's roll about once again.

They do. **LV** *above, still in corner with blankets grabbed to her.*

LV (*in a whisper*) Dad, Dad, Dad, Dad, Dad, Dad, Dad.

Below **Ray** *and* **Mari** *fall off settee.*

Mari I'm going go up and have a word with her. I feel tight.

She stands up with difficulty and heads for stairs.

Ray Aye and I'm off an' all to rustle up some champagne.

Mari At this time?

Ray Sure.

Mari Nowt's beyond you Ray is it? You're a bloody genius in your own right.

Ray Hey, how about some takeaway an all.

Mari Ooh yeah. I'll have a Kwai Chang Caine with curry, rice and chips.

Ray Okay. Hey, I wanna just be sure of one thing. She'll be there, won't she Mari?

Mari Leave it wi' me Ray. I know her. I am her mother after all.

Ray Soy sauce?

Mari *puts up the 'OK' sign.*

Ray *blows her a drunken kiss.* **Mari** *catches it and spreads it all over her face and neck.*

He leaves. She goes upstairs.

LV *hears someone on the stairs. Quickly she throws pillow under sheet like she's there, then runs out room and into bathroom.* **Mari** *comes quietly into room, in dark, just moonlight through window. She sits on end of bed.*

Mari I know you can't be asleep yet our LV, but I won't make you sit up. I don't like forcing you into something like this, I know it's against your nature, but your Mam's sick of struggling, love. Sick to the bones with working and still having nowt. I'm thinking of you as well, you can't go on like this forever, stuck in your room, you're young. You have to do something with your life. This might bring you out, eh? Eh? You don't know what it could lead to, eh? You've always been a little voice and you've never liked much, to speak and such, but this thing you've developed could make us Ray reckons. Don't know where the hell it's come from, such a small quiet lonely thing you've always been. I could almost fit you in my two hands as a babe. (*Cups her two hands.*) I don't know if it's the drink but I keep seeing you tonight as our little LV there, little pale chil' in me arms, or in the old pram there, that lemon coloured crocheted blanket around you, tiny good-as-gold face in the wool. I'm sorry for the way I am love at times with you, it seems to be the way I am. It seems to be something . . . Anyway think on it, our LV. You will won't you, eh? Eh?

She reaches over and gently touches lump. Touches it again. Jumps up, pulls cover back. Grabs up cushion.

Mari The little piss. I'll have her.

She head butts the cushion splitting it and sending feathers everywhere. **Ray** *enters below, bottle in one hand, takeaway in the other, slamming door.* **LV** *comes out from bathroom, then looks towards her room in fright.* **Mari** *spins round to see her, shouting through the feather fall.*

Mari YOU ARE BLOODY DOING IT!

Blackout.

Interval.

Act Two

The club.

The organ and drums duo are playing frantically away at full blast.

Mr Boo *comes on, the music stops with a cymbals clash.*

Mr Boo Tar. Thank you. Tar. (*Indicates organist.*) Jean on her organ, ladies and gentlemen, Jean.

Mr Boo *applauds.* **Jean** *plays a riff.*

Mr Boo Jean, lovely. And Manolito, ladies and gentlemen, Manolito.

He plays a bit of drums. **Mr Boo** *applauds, riff continues as he speaks.*

Mr Boo Yes. Yes. Beat that meat, Manolito. Yes sir. Bad man, bad.

He does a little Michael Jackson dance. Manolito ends riff. **Mr Boo** *steps forward to audience.*

Mr Boo Yes. Here we are. Here we are then.

Mr Boo *at mike.*

Mr Boo Boo here. Don't shout my name too loud or I'll think you don't like me. How you all doing, alreet?! (*Waits for audience response.*) Come on you can do better than that. How you all doing?! Alreet. Great. Now then, now then, as you know, Boo braves anything, goes anywhere in his perpetual quest to hunt down fresh talent and lay it at your mercy. And you know how I've sweated, and you know how I've toiled, and you know how I've bent over backwards. (*To someone in* *audience.*) Watch it! And you know I've left no tonsil unturned in my unceasing search for something new on the vocal front. But for all that, I've found her round the corner, on the doorstep, at the kitchen table, she's so local I could spit and hit her. A talent, an undiscovered treasure. An act of wonder, ladies and gentlemen, something to thrill to, to spill beer or tears to, a little girl that's big, a northern light, a rising star, order and hush, hush and order, for the turn of turns. The one, the only, LITTLE VOICE! LITTLE VOICE!

Spotlight burning the stage. Microphone on stand. **Ray** *brings* **LV** *halfway on, directs her towards microphone, leaves. She comes into spot. She stands there. Quiet. Stands there. Quiet, trembling. Opens her mouth. Nothing. Upset.*

Ray's voice Lights, turn the lights out!

All the lights go out. She sings: Billy Holiday 'Lover Man'. Perfect impersonation. After a few lines, suddenly stops abruptly.

Ray's voice Do another, do another, more.

She does 'Chicago' Judy Garland. After a verse or so, again cuts off.

Ray's voice What you stopped for? Don't stop now. Do anything, anything.

She sings 'Happy Birthday' Marilyn Monroe. Finishes.

Ray's voice Get 'em back up! Back up!

Lights up. She is caught 'feeling it' then stunned like a frightened animal caught in headlights.

Blackout.

Lights up. Bam.

Back at house. **LV** *in her room.* **Mari** *downstairs, going frantically about the place throwing things over her shoulder, looking for something.*

Ray *at table, paper and pen out, working excitedly.*

Mari Embarrassing!

Throws something without looking. It just misses **Ray**, *who doesn't even respond, just ducks and carries on working.*

Mari Bloody one hundred chunk embarrassing that. I'm shown up. I'll never place my face in there again. Never, never. (*To* **Ray**.) Will you stop that scritching. I've just been involved with the worst spectacle and frig-up in Mari's history and you're crouched there scritching like a rat.

Ray I'm working on the act.

Mari Working on the act. Working on the act. Are you mental altogether? What act! There was only one sucker on show there tonight, me! Embarrassing. See her quavering in the dark there like a demic! See her! And what was she singing? What the hell was that? She could a made an effort and done Kylie for Christsake.

Ray Calm down.

Mari Calm down! You must be jesting. I'm up to me neck in shame.

Ray We had to find her limits. See what she could do.

Mari Nowt.

Ray No. The gold's there alright. I've just got to find me a way of fetching it out.

Mari Frig that. (*Returns to searching.*) Is there not a bottle nowhere?

Ray If the artiste won't go to the act, the act will have to go to the artiste. All's I have to do is think. Get my mind out, think.

Mari You should a thunk before. You wouldn't listen, would you? I told you and bloody Boo Lou, both, you were wasting your time on the slit. She did the whole thing on purpose to spite mother. I know her Ray. Oh my God, when she come on like that though. Oh my God. I din't know where to put meself. I still don't. Shame ran right up me leg.

Suddenly there's a sound like stones hitting a window. We see **Billy** *in the alley under the lamp, tossing little stones up to* **LV**'s *window.*

Mari What's that? Is that in my head or on the outside?

Ray Eh? What? (*He listens.*) Outside.

Mari Bam me, funny business!

She bursts out of the house and sees **Billy.**

Mari Clear off. Go on. Heated up pole. Piss it. Go.

He's gone. She throws stones after him. **Mari** *goes back in.*

Mari I'm too mad to live tonight.

She looks this way and that for something to grab. She turns on **Ray** *who's still working.*

Mari Anyway, stop that off! Cause she's not doing another. No way. Don't forget that's my diddy and

delicate daughter you're twiddling wi'. And besides that
there's my personal mother's nerves to consider!

He grabs her quickly by the wrist and pulls her onto his knee.

Ray (*quickly*) Come here. Calm down!

He starts tickling her up and down.

Ray Calm down. Calm down.

She starts hooting and laughing.

Mari Stop it. Oooooo. Stop it.

Ray (*tickling on*) You're calming down now, eh?
Calming down now, eh?

He stops. She remains on his lap.

Ray You calmed down now, eh? Eh?

Mari Oh but Ray, it were crap awful weren't it, and
you're on about putting us through it again.

Ray Mari, it's there, believe me. She's not a performer,
I'll admit, no, but I can take care of that. Bear with me
dove, while I work out the last details. I'm only
gripping on to it so tight Mari, so pit bull tight, for all
of us, cause I know it can take us to the top.

Mari Oooh. I love it when you talk swanky.

Ray If you knew how long I've been looking for
summat like this. And here it is in me lap. (*Quickly.*)
Along with you, along with you.

*She giggles and buries her head in him. As she does he quickly
writes more on the paper.*

Ray Aye. Aye

Mari *comes back up.*

Mari You really is gone on this, ain't you Ray?

Ray I am dove, I've never had nowt decent to set meself on before, scrap, bent bookying, a bit o' this and that, clapped out old acts and knackered strippers.

Mari Don't. Don't do yoursen down Ray. You're Elvis in my eyes.

Ray Okay, granted, I might be the King of this gutter in which we live. But what's that? There's stuff above, love. Bungalows, gravel drives, Chateau Niff on tap, teeing off with Tarbuck and Brucie.

Mari Ooooh, hey. (*Sings.*) I did it my Ray. Oh there were times, I've had a few, bit off, bit off . . .

Ray Aye, aye, Mari. (*Shoving her off his lap.*) I've just got make a quick call.

She stands up.

Mari Okay, man o' mine, frigging go for it and you can depend on me. One hundred pesetas. In fact, I'll drink to that.

She goes off, still singing to herself, hunting for booze.

Ray (*through on phone*) Hello. Hello. 'Tape-deck', is that you? Yep, it's Ray. I'm calling in that favour you owe me . . .

Mari *is still singing and chucking stuff about at the back.*

Ray (*covers phone*) Mari, Mari. Here, look, here, (*Holding out a fiver.*) go down the offy.

Mari Ray, you're speaking my very language again. Tar.

She takes it, tries kissing him, phone wire getting caught up, etc.

Ray (*pulling away*) Aye.

Mari See you later, Ray-ver.

Ray Aye. Aye.

Mari (*leaving, stops at open door for an exit line.*
Overcome) Sometimes, suddenly, life's nowt but holy
in' it?

She goes. Pause. **Ray** *remains, looking at closed door in
disbelief. Then turns back out front.*

Ray (*to himself*) Bloody hell. (*Back on phone.*) Meet me
tomorrow down the club, okay. Bring your stuff. Just
be there.

Puts phone down. Carries on scribbling.

Billy *appears in alley again, with a lamp, and shines light up
into* **LV**'s *room, turning it on and off.* **LV** *comes to window.
Opens it to see what's outside.*

Billy Over here. It's me.

LV Eh?

Billy Billy. LV, I've just been down the club after
hours, to weigh up the space an all that for the light
show. I got a shock. I saw 'Little Voice' on a turn
poster, singing impressionist. Is it you?

LV You have lights. I have voices.

Billy Voices?

LV I sing in these voices. I . . . I hardly know I do it.
It's just for me. Comfort. I . . . I . . .

Billy Hey, say no more LV. That's enough for me. I
understand. But why you doing it down there?

LV They made me.

Billy Who made you?

LV Him and her. They go on until you do.

Billy Can't you say 'owt to make them see?

LV No one never listens to anybody but themselves, too loud.

Billy I do.

LV Yes.

Billy Are they trying to make you do it again?

LV She didn't like it. I won't be doing it no more.

Billy Oh well, that's good in it?

She nods.

Billy You do what's right for you Little Voice.

She nods.

Billy And cheer up.

She smiles.

LV Talk about the lights.

Billy Well, space down there is big enough. And it got me going. Aye, me brain came on straight away, making lights. Having a do wi' the dark. (*As though he's in the space.*) I thought, here, fwun. (*He swings his torch out over the audience in a beam of light.*) There, (*Swings beam in another direction, across audience, making a sound like a bullet.*) pkooo. (*Another direction.*) Here, zhum. (*Stops.*) I saw all sorts. It'll take some time though to fix it all up. Bloke said I can make a start any night as long as it's after hours. I don't know though. Would you be coming down? You never said you see.

LV I . . . .

She hears footsteps on stairs.

Billy What's up?

LV Oo somebody's coming. I got go now, will you come again, Billy?

Billy Yeah soon, soon as I can.

She quickly pulls window down and sits on bed.

Ray *knocks on door. Goes in.*

Ray LV, I've worked out the new act. You'll love it. Everything tailored to your personality. All you have to do is step on from the side.

She looks away.

Ray What's the matter? Hey, don't let a little hiccup like tonight put you off. Could happen to anyone.

LV Don't want do another.

Ray Listen, could happen to the best of them that. (*Pointing at albums.*) If you could ask her or her or her they'd tell you the same. They've had them nights an' all. Haven't you, Judy? (*Answering in her voice.*) 'I sure have Mr Say.' (*Laughs.*) How about you, Marilyn? 'Yes Ray, boo be do.'

LV Don't.

Ray Seriously, it'll never happen again, not with this LV. (*Showing paper.*) It's foolproof. Believe me. Let's do it eh?

LV *shakes her head.*

Ray Won't you even look at it?

LV *shakes her head.*

Ray Well, if that's what you want. (*Folds paper in half.*)

LV 'Tis.

Ray Okay. But it's a shame to just leave it like that.
How about just giving it a try, just once LV. (*Holds up a
digit.*) One more time and if it don't work out we'll
forget it forever. I'll leave you to your records and your
room.

She shakes her head.
Ray *folds paper again.*

Ray Fair enough, I've got me other acts, I'll be alright.
I'll survive, so will you, it's just that . . . (*Looks at folded
paper.*) Well never mind. Never mind then. That's that.

He folds paper completely and puts it in his back pocket.

Ray Aye, you've got it nice in here ain't you? Clean
and tidy. (*Sits on her bed.*) All your records round you.
(*Looks.*) Your Dad must a spent years building up this
collection.

LV He did.

Ray I were never one for collecting things myself, only
debts, I had an Auntie who was though. You'll never
guess what she collected, go on.

LV What?

Ray Bluebirds. Wild bluebirds. Flying all round her
house. Marvellous with 'em she was. You know she
even got one of 'em to talk once. Yeah. Timid little
thing it was, no bigger than your thumb, too scared to
even leave its cage. And the way she did it were so
simple. All she did was keep it shaded and safe at all
times, sing to it, while stroking it, very soft, every day.
And after a while it gave her its heart. And later, when
it had grown strong, she set it free, but before it left, it
stopped on the window ledge, turned, and to her great

surprise sang. (*Sings.*) 'There'll be bluebirds over, the white cliffs of Dover, tomorrow . . .' See there she goes.

They both watch, as though they see it fly away. **Ray** *taps* **LV**, *and smiles.*

Ray Eh, true that.

Ray *gently reaches down and picks up an album from a nearby pile.*

Ray Beautifully taken care of these, the covers and all that. Are you carrying on keeping 'em the same?

LV He showed me.

Ray Yeah, wiping 'em before play 'an all that?

She nods.

Ray Good thing. Collector's items some of them I imagine. Which were his favourites?

LV Them four there. (*Points to a pile.*)

Ray Ahh. (*Goes in pocket for paper, gets it out.*) Oh no.

LV What?

Ray Well. I was thinking we could a made sure we'd got them in, but we're not doing it now. (*Puts paper back.*)

LV Oh.

Ray Bet he would a liked that though, your Dad, eh? Tribute to his life's love performed by his only daughter. That would a been something wun't it eh? Sounds like he deserved it too. He were a good un eh, your Dad?

LV *nods.*

Ray I bet. Shame. Cause let's face it, the man and his music don't get much respect do they (*indicating downstairs*), if you know what I mean.

LV Ray.

Ray (*expectant*) Yeah?

LV Nothing.

Ray (*thrown, then . . .*) Look, there she goes again, the bluebird, under the moon and over the stars.

LV I'll do it.

Ray (*casually*) Oh, okay.

LV Only once.

Ray (*still casual, containing himself, not looking at her. Begins to leave*) Right then. I'm pleased. I'll just nip downstairs for me ciggies, back in a sec.

He goes halfway downstairs, stops. Faces out. Then, like a bastard.

Ray (*to himself*) Yes! Yes! Yes!

Blackout.

Lights up. The evening of the performance. **Sadie** *is helping to dress* **LV** *in* **LV**'s *room. Quietly, caringly.* **Sadie** *has a fancy blouse on from 1964 or thereabouts, with ruffled frontage. She zips up* **LV**, *who is in a long, to the ground, incredible, figure-hugging, glittering, showbusiness dress.*

Suddenly **Mari** *comes bursting out of her room, struggling to do herself up.*

Mari SADIE! SADIE, come here. Where are you when I need you, frig!

Mari *carries on down to bottom of stairs, still struggling.*
Sadie *comes out the room and down.*

Mari SADIE!

Sadie *arrives.*

Mari Oh thank God for that, I need fastening up. It's harder and harder to get into this stuff, I tell you.

Sadie *does it for her.*

Mari Oh tar, well done Sadie, tar, here have a sherry for your accomplishments. Set you up for tonight as well.

Sadie Okay.

Mari Pour me one while you're at it.

Sadie Okay.

Sadie *pours two.* **Mari** *preens and lacquers her hair.*

Mari Fair old frontage on the blouse there Sade, eh?

Sadie *nods. Sits and sips her sherry.*

Mari You looking forward to going down there tonight then, Sadie? Yes. You stick with me, I'll make sure no one laughs at you.

Mari *lacquers more.*

Mari Ray's worked it all out. He thinks he's taking us all to Tarbyland. I had me doubts about her doing it again but, well he's won me over. I can't say no to him. Oh what a tongue that guy has, half raspberry, half razor.

Lacquers more.

Mari And I don't know, maybe for once that fucker fate is smiling down on us. How do you feel, Sade?

Sadie *and* **Mari** Okay.

Sadie Dokey.

Mari See, see. (*She carries on preening.*) There's certainly some raspberry in the air from somewhere. Oh, sod the devil, I'll put some bit more cheeks on.

She leans into mirror, putting make-up on.

Ray *comes in silently without her noticing. Puts sssh sign up to* **Sadie**. *Creeps up behind* **Mari** *with a necklace open ready to put round her neck. Just at that moment,* **Mari** *suddenly sprays lacquer, it goes all in* **Ray**'s *eyes.*

Ray Bloody hell. Aarrgh!

Mari Sorry. Oh my God. I've blinded my God. Oh no!

Ray *shutting and scrunching up his eyes.*

Ray I'm alright. I'm alright. Here, I got you something.

Holds out necklace.

Mari Oh, Raymondo, oh, oh. Look here, Sadie. (*Holds it to her neck.*) Fasten it for me, sir.

Ray Er. (*Hands out, then, finding something to wipe his eyes.*) I'm not coming near you.

Mari I'll do it then. (*She does.*) Looky here. Little sparkle neck me. See Sade. A love token. That's it in it, Ray?

Ray *nods.*

Mari In some ways, wish I could lash it round me finger. Ha.

Holds up engagement finger.

Ray (*to* **Sadie**) Well now Sadie, you're looking beautiful tonight love. Are we gonna get a dance down there tonight then. Eh?

Sadie *laughing.*

Mari (*quickly in*) Sadie, go upstairs now, see if she's ready, the star.

Sadie *does.*

Ray Can't wait Mari, can you? I'm buzzing fit to bust. Are you?

Mari (*unsure*) Yeah.

Ray What's up wi' you?

Mari Oh X-Ray, you can see right through me, can't you? It's just, what the sod hell are we to expect tonight?

Ray Mari. Mari, dove. Don't you worry 'bout a thing. All you have to do is be your radiant self as always.

Mari Aaay, Dr Ray, you can make me better with just a look and a word

She goes to kiss him but as she does, **LV** *appears on stairs.* **Ray** *moves away from* **Mari**.

Ray Aye, yes, hey, here she comes!

Sadie *brings* **LV** *down.* **LV** *dressed for performance. She is blank faced and looking 'not there'.*

Mari Aye, here she is.

Ray Let me open that door. The door that leads to success.

Ray *gets door.* **Sadie** *slips a plastic mac on* **LV***'s shoulders.*

Mari Hey, get Sadie, the minder. (*She does a karate chop.*)

They set to leave in a procession almost. **LV** *looking down,* **Sadie** *behind her,* **Ray** *and then* **Mari**.

Mari And looky here, LV. (*Prinks necklace.*) Prink, prink. (*As they leave.*) As we leave, star spangling down the club, the artiste, the minder, the manager and the Mum.

Door bangs behind them. Lights of the house flicker, flicker but remain on.

Blackout.

The club. **Mr Boo** *at the mike.*

Mr Boo Testing, testing. Mr Boo here. Don't say my name too loud you'll give me a fright. No, now then. Ladies and gentlemen, forgive me if I get serious for a moment, what do you mean I never got funny? No, we've a return act for tonight, 'Little Voice'. I think you'll agree that last time the voice was there but the rest was little. Now I know we're a tough club, a hard club, and proud of it. And acts fall like flies in here. But I put in a plea if I dare for this girl. I put in a request if I may, for a bit of order, a little support if you could people, for the girl with the greats queueing in her gullet, shy little, Little Voice, ladies and gentlemen. Little Voice Hoff from down our way.

Ray *brings on a blindfolded* **LV** *and leads her to the centre of the stage. He turns her upstage, her back to the audience and* *removes the blindfold. He steps away. Signals for the music to begin. Exits.*

Orchestration of 'Goldfinger' begins. **LV** *slowly turns around. Sings abbreviated versions of the following songs:*

Shirley Bassey – 'Goldfinger'. (One verse.)

Shirley Bassey – 'Big Spender'.

Marilyn Monroe – 'I Wanna Be Loved By You'.

Gracie Fields – 'Sing As We Go'.

Edith Piaf – 'No Regrets'.

Judy Garland – 'Get Happy'. (With a big finish.)

Music ends. **LV** *in arms up, Garland pose. Blackout.*

Lights up.

They all burst in. **Mari** *first, then* **Ray***, then* **Boo***,* **LV** *and* **Sadie***. They have loads of booze with them.*

Ray What about that, then?

Starts opening drinks. **Sadie** *gets* **LV** *to the settee and sits her down.*

Mr Boo Marvellous. Oh my God. Tears down cheeks.

Mari *screaming out.*

Ray See 'em all standing up. (*Imitates applause.*)

Mari *screaming out.*

Ray Here we go. (*Popping a shaken beer can, spraying everywhere.*) Ale and everything all round.

They all get into the drinks, except **LV** *alone on settee, staring out.*

Mr Boo Well, Ray, I can safely say your booking's assured down there. And have you, have you ever thought of the Monaco Club?

Ray Well, yes. Bloody, yes. Hey, Mari, we might be doing the Monaco Club an' all.

Mari *screaming. She puts the Jackson 5 on. Starts jiving with* **Sadie,** *who just remains standing still, with one arm out, while* **Mari** *does it.* **Sadie** *looks ill.*

Ray (*to* **Mr Boo**) Oh yes, Monaco for a bit, Mr Boo, I'll not say no, at this stage who would? But you know as well as me that soon not even the Monaco is going to be big enough for this.

LV, *exhausted, hears this, starts shaking her head. No one can see.*

Ray Mr Boo . . .

Mr Boo Do call me Lou.

Ray Mr Boo . . .

Mr Boo Lou.

Ray Lou, let me tell you. This is the greatest act going, this. We'll be in London before Christmas, or the cruises or the telly. Take it, take it from me.

LV (*shaking her head*) Once . . .

Mr Boo I hear what you're saying there Ray. But I hope you'll not forget where you got your start.

LV Once was said.

Mr Boo What was that, LV? What's she on about? I can't hear her.

Ray *is popping another bottle.*

Ray Is Sadie alright?

Mr Boo *looks too.* **Sadie** *looks a bit ill, and vacant, staring out.* **Mari** *stops dancing on* **Sadie***'s arm, and looks at her. Then to* **Ray***.*

Mari Sadie, Sadie May! She's alright. She's alright, aren't you?

She slaps **Sadie** *on the back,* **Sadie** *hiccups at this.* **Mari** *goes towards bottle* **Ray** *is holding, they all turn away to pour.* **Sadie** *has a little dribbly sick down her blouse. But just remains standing where she is.*

Ray We on for the whole week then, Lou?

Mr Boo It's yours Ray.

.LV passes out.

Mr Boo I've cancelled the Silverados and Gringo Hodges to have it free for you. I couldn't do nothing else, they were going mad in there.

Ray I know.

Mr Boo Wouldn't leave me alone.

Ray I know. I saw.

Mr Boo 'When?' 'When's she on again?' and all that.

Ray *(drinks)* Yes. Yesssss!

Mr Boo *(to* **Mari***)* You must be proud, Mrs Hoff.

Mari *screams.*

Ray By the way, Sadie's been sick.

Mari Oh, bloody hell. (*To* **Sadie**.) Sadie! Sink and wipe. Sink and wipe.

Sadie *moves off on her own in direction of sink.* **Mari** *pours herself another.*

Mr Boo Well, Ray. (*Lifting glass.*) To the rise of Little Voice.

Ray (*raising his glass.*) Up tut' sky. Up tut' bloody sky.

Mari *turns just in time to lift her glass to join the others.*

Ray Cheers!

Mr Boo Cheers!

Phone rings. **Mari** *picks phone up. Screams down it. Puts it back down. Turns to see* **LV** *has passed out on settee. Looks again.*

Mari What's this. RAY! RAY!

Ray *comes over.*

Mari Oh God, has the little bird bleated and died wi' all the shock!

Ray She's alright. Just the excitement, that's all.

Mr Boo Loosen her clothes around the throat.

Ray *starts to loosen* **LV**'*s clothes.*

Mari (*stopping him*) I'll do that.

She tries but is fumbling, too drunk. **Sadie** *comes through, lifts* **LV** *and starts to carry her slowly upstairs.*

Mari (*taken aback*) Oh, aye, tar, Sadie.

Sadie *goes slowly upstairs.* **Ray**, **Mari** *and* **Mr Boo** *watching in silence, not moving, for as long as it takes for* **Sadie** *to carry her to her room.*

Mr Boo 'Blessed are the meek for they shall inherit the earth.' When, eh, when?

Ray Eh?

Mari *turns the record player back up.*

The lights blow.

Blackout.

Some days later. Evening. Alley lit by lamp only. **Billy** *is crouching there with a lamp, shining it on and off through her window. No response.*

Billy LV.

Flashes light.

LV.

Flashes light.

You're there.

Flashes light.

I know you're there.

Flashes light.

Can't you see me light? I've come every night since we last spoke.

Flashes light.

I'm worried. I know they're making you do it again and again and again. Are you alright?

Flashes light. Flashes light, almost like a morse code. No response.

The lights LV, I've gone ahead and started setting up. Getting stuff down. So much is needed.

Flashes light.

LV. I feel you flickering, fading away. I don't know how, it's like when one of my lights is ready to go, I feel it, I just know.

Flashes light, really fast one after another. No response. Starts to flash slow, slow again.

I know if I can get you to the lights they'll lift you. I know they will because I'm doing it for you. I've not said that to you yet, but I'm doing them for you.

Flashes light.

LV.

Flashes light.

LV. LV.

I'll not leave you, I'll be back.

He gives up, turns light slowly down, as lights come slowly up on next scene.

Lights up on living room. Some days later (same evening as the last scene), the evening of a performance. **LV** *is in her room in bed. All around her unopened presents. Bouquets of flowers beginning to fade. Downstairs,* **Mari** *sits on settee, looking out, drinking.* **Sadie** *is slowly making sandwiches on the kitchen table. Silence, except for the soft sound of sandwiches being made.* **Mari** *drinks.*

Sadie *works.* **Sadie** *finishes, puts last sandwich on plate, and begins to set off upstairs with them. As she passes* **Mari**.

Mari Here, give us them Sadie. I'll take 'em up.

Mari *takes tray and goes upstairs. Goes in* **LV**'s *room.*

Mari LV, love.

LV *is under covers, won't come out.*

Mari Come on, you can't stay there all day and night. I've brought you something to eat, you've got to eat, you've not ate now for four days. What about I put some music on then, some of your music, see what you think, eh?

LV *gives no response.* **Mari** *lifts the sandwiches above her head like she's going to throw them down.*

Mari I ready to throw these butties all over you. I will, you know I will.

She stares down, no movement. She sadly puts them on table by her and leaves.

Downstairs the phone rings. **Sadie** *answers it tentatively, unused to it, she listens.*

Sadie Hello. Okay . . . Okay! . . . OKAY!!

Mari *has arrived from upstairs.*

Mari That'll be Auntie. Pass it here. Auntie Slit, it's me Mari . . . No, I am Mari. Bloody hell. What? Yes. Yes she's on stage now Auntie, can you believe it? No you can't . . . Well it's right, our shy little LV is in showbizliness. I know what you're thinking. How long can it go on, well this is her fourth spot at the club and it's going down a treat and a malteser. Really, really, really they love her. Oh, I think so. Yes, she's fine, FINE! But you know what she's like. Anyway, tar for concern Aunt. Must dash now, yes. Woof woof. See you.

Mari *puts phone down and turns to* **Sadie**.

Mari She won't touch 'em, Sadie. She's not touched anything else we've left either, cup of stone cold tea there. She's on soon. She'll have to bloody go. I wonder if we're pushing her too hard, you know. One show after another. She'll not die, Sadie, will she? Die off? She's only frail, you know, like her Father was before her. Have a to ring Doctor Sock? I don't know. I'll wait for Ray, he'll be here in a minute. I don't know what to do any more. Come and sit by me, Sadie.

Sadie *does*.

Mari Look at me. Am I a good mother, am I doing right? I mean, she's making money now, I mean it's setting her off on something. In the long run, she'll thank me for it, won't she? There's always suffering and struggle in't there, and then they make it in the end. I've cheered up now. Tar for t'advice, Sadie. Don't know what I'd do without you. (*Half to herself*.) You patient fat get.

The phone rings.

She picks it up. **Sadie** *heads for stairs.* **Mari** *covers mouthpiece.*

Mari Are you going up for a go?

Sadie *nods.* **Mari** *nods.* **Mari** *speaks into phone.*

Mari Hello. Oh is that the local rag? (*Goes posh*.) No, no, she's not available for interviews, best try tomorrow, thanking you.

Puts phone down.

Mari Now then.

Door opens. **Ray** *comes in. Looking more affluent. He is smoking a cigar.*

Mari Darling.

She throws her arms round him.

Ray Alright Mari, alright. Where is she?

Mari Ray?

Ray Yeah.

Mari Er, don't know how to . . .

Ray What?

Mari Can she not have this night off?

Ray Not tonight, no. I've got Bunny Morris coming to see her, this could be a proper break. This could even mean telly.

Mari Telly?

Ray Telly.

Mari *runs to mirror and pokes her hair about.* **Ray** *goes to kettle.*

Mari Telly?

Ray Telly.

Ray *plugs kettle in, it flashes.*

You wanna watch that! Bugger me.

He rinses out a cup, has a drink of water.

Mari Ray . . .

Ray Yeah.

Mari Er, don't know how to . . .

Ray What?

Mari Any money sorted yet? I've only had a five and your dead Mam's necklace.

Ray Mari, I keep saying, leave it with me, it's all being carefully proportioned. Me and Boo is in fact just finalising a new contract. I'll let you read it when it's done.

Mari Oh no, no, no need for that. Just lob the doubloons into me open handbag when they's ready.

Ray Right then. You picked up them dresses from the dry cleaners, din't you?

Mari Oh.

Ray Don't tell me what I think you're going to tell me, please don't.

Mari *opening and closing her mouth like a fish, not knowing what to do.*

Ray Don't.

Mari *continues fish.*

Ray You forgot, din't you?

Mari *nods.*

Ray Oh no!

Mari I've been so busied, Ray.

Ray Bloody hell.

He boots the pouffe.

Mari Hey, watch me furniture!

Ray She's on any minute.

Mari I know! I know! Oh so sorry darling.

Goes to embrace him.

Don't be crossy wid your rolling puss puss.

Ray Never mind all that, she'll have to wear one of her old ones.

Mari Yes. Yes she must.

Ray What's she got?

Mari What's she got? What's she got? I don't know.

Ray Ooh!

Mari SADIE! (*Suddenly remembers.*) Wait a minute, I think there's one in the dirty wash.

Ray Bloody hell!

Mari It's alright, I'll iron it.

She gets dress out. Tries putting the ironing board up and nearly kills herself. **Sadie** *has arrived by this time. She and* **Ray** *watch in amazement.*

Mari Save me, Sadie! Save me.

Sadie Okay.

Sadie *takes over the ironing.* **Mari** *goes to* **Ray**.

Mari Ray Milland, you still my friend, an't you? Eh? Eh?

Ray We can't have this, Mari. I'm going to have to get someone else to look after her.

Mari What you on about, I'm her Mother.

Ray Are you?

Mari Yes. And you're my man.

Ray Am I?

Mari Ray, Ray, what you saying?

He walks away. She turns, kicks something flying, then turns to **Sadie**.

Mari You're too quiet to be my friend, you. Fuck off.

Sadie *goes.* **Mari** *picks iron up and starts ironing. She is slipping all over the place.*

Mari I'm doing it now, Ray love. Yes I am. I'll flatten it just so, once I've got me legs right.

Ray Leave it, you're gonna get burnt in a minute.

Mari *carries on frantically ironing, trying.*

Ray LEAVE IT!

She stops. Pause. He goes and gets dress.

Ray It'll have to do.

He is about to walk away, she grabs his hand.

Mari (*pleading*) Ray.

Ray Leave it, Mari.

Mari You're always rushing away, Ray.

Ray There's a lot to do.

Mari Ray, kiss me.

She strains towards him.

Ray Oh, get off.

Mari Ray?

Ray (*getting away*) Stop clinging on me!

Mari (*coming close again*) Don't spoil it, Ray! We go together so well.

Ray Go together well! Go to . . . Don't kid yourself woman, we go nowhere. For a start, you're past it, your body's gone. When your clothes go, I can't keep track of it, it's all over the place. Too many maulings, Mari. And you're too loud and you stink of drink. That's alright for where you belong, the alley wall, the back of a car, flat on your back on a rug. But no way could you come with me and her to better things. No way love. Look at yourself, look, lumping out your crazy clothes, just about keeping your balance. Christ do you think I don't have birds I go to, do you not think it's like putting my face in flowers after you. You've had it Mari, you're nowt now but something for after the boozer, a chaser, a takeaway, a bit of a laugh. All you've ever had that I want sits up there. And all you're doing is getting in the way, woman. You were in the way the night I heard her, that night I heard her singing, and you're still in the way now. For godsake wise up and fuck off.

He grabs up the dress and rushes upstairs. **Mari** *is shattered, arms out in front, like a drunk lost thing, broken. Reaching out, she walks out the door almost in a trance.*

Mari Sadie. Sadie. Sadie.

Ray *has arrived upstairs.* **LV** *is still in the bed.*

Ray Here, get this on, we're late. Come on. Come on. I've had enough of you lot tonight.

LV *doesn't respond.*

Ray Dress on.

She doesn't respond.

Ray Get this on.

He grabs her up. She's limp in his hand. He slaps her. At that, voices begin to rush out of her uncontrollably, some sung, some spoken.

Judy Garland (JG), Piaf (P), Marilyn Monroe (MM), Shirley Bassey (SB), Billie Holiday (BH), Cilla Black (CB), Gracie Fields (GF).

LV (BH) 'Stop haunting me now, just leave me alone.' (SB) 'This is my life.'

Ray Hey.

LV (JG) Toto, Toto.

Ray Stop it.

LV (SB) 'Let me live. Oh let me live.'

Ray Stop it, I'm warning you!

LV (MM) 'Look what you started, a conflagration baby, that's what.' (SB) 'But if you go I won't cry.'

Ray Stop this.

LV (BH) 'You go your way and I go mine, it's best that we do.'

Ray Save it for tonight.

LV (SB) 'I, I, who have nothing, I, I who have no one.' (MM) 'But my heart belongs to Daddy.'

Ray Damn you LV.

Ray *is backing off a bit now with the sheer force of it.*

LV (CB) 'Something tells me, something's gonna happen tonight.'

Ray Oh no.

LV (JG) 'If you let me, let me, let me.' (SB) 'With my hands pressed up against the window pane.'

Ray Not mad. Not now please.

LV (P) 'Da Da Da Da Da Da . . .'

Ray Don't crack now, LV. Noo!

LV (P) '. . . Da Da Da Da Da Da.' Encore milord.

Ray No.

LV (MM) I'm tired of getting the fuzzy end of the lollipop.

Ray Please LV!

LV (JG) You go away or I'll bite you myself.
(SB) 'This is me. This is me.'

Ray Is it too late? Come back!

LV (JG) 'I guess when you met me it was just one of those things.'

Ray Oh my god. Come wi' me.

Ray *beckons to her.*

LV (SB) 'Beckons you to enter his web of sin, but don't go in.' (P) 'For at last I happen to be strong.'

Ray *is knocked back onto his knees.*

Ray I pray you LV. We was on our way together.

LV (JG) 'Happy together, unhappy together.'
(MM) See what I mean, not very bright. (JG) 'I'm going to haunt you so, I'm going to taunt you so, I'm going to drive you to ruin.'

Spins around and knocks **Ray** *who falls downstairs. He holds his mouth.*

Ray Me teeth.

LV (GF) Never mind your teeth, leave 'em out.

Ray *is at bottom of stairs. He looks up, she is still going from voice to voice, oblivious.*

LV (JG) 'Zing, zing, zing.'

She goes back in her room.

LV (CB) 'Step inside love, and stay, Step inside love, step inside love.' (SB) 'Just an empty room, full of empty space, like the empty look I see on your face.' (GF) 'Sally, Sally, pride of our alley.'

Ray, *devastated, rushes out, slams the door. With the force of the slam, the iron falls off the ironing board. Socket explodes. Light cracks and a flame rips around the ceiling and wall sides. A fire begins.* **LV** *in her room, still going from one voice to another.*

(JG) Run Toto, run Toto. He got away. He got away. (P) Bravo, bravo.

The sound of fire below, smoke is rising and into the room. She is oblivious to it. Smoke almost covering her.

LV (JG) 'Cos when you're crying, don't you know that your make-up starts to run, and your eyes get red and scrappy.' (P) 'Both the good and the bad I have flung in the fire.' (MM) 'But baby I like it hot.' (JG) 'Glory, glory, hallelujah, glory, glory, hallelujah, his truth is marching on.' (JG) I'm frightened Auntie Em, I'm frightened. (JG) There's no place like home. There's no place like home. There's no place like home. There's no place like home . . . .

Suddenly the 'Cherry Picker' appears high in the alley and glides up to the window. **Billy** *is in it. He breaks the window with his hammer, opens it and gets her out. Still she is going from voice to voice as the machine takes them away and down the alley.*

Blackout.

The club is packed. **Mr Boo** *excited and worried. His toupee on tilt. Sweat pouring off him. Caught in mid-speech . . .*

Mr Boo Calm down. Calm down. Sorry she's late. She'll be here any minute. I assure you. Look, sit down at the back! I never thought we could get so many in. What a star turn eh! Calm down. She'll be here soon! (*To someone.*) Look stop that! (*To someone.*) Put that back woman!

Suddenly, the opening strains of the song 'It's Over', Roy Orbison, come on from the juke box.

Mr Boo Hey get that bloody juke box off! Who's put that on.

Ray *comes toward stage.* **Boo** *sees him.*

Mr Boo Ray Say's here.

Ray *comes straight on, grabs the mike without looking at* **Boo** *and walks to centre stage,* **Boo** *following him.*

Mr Boo Where is she Ray? Where is she?

Ray *pushes him away.*

Mr Boo Hey, who you shoving. (*Sees something's up.*) What you playing at, give me that.

Reaching for mike.

Mr Boo Here.

Ray *suddenly threatens him, very violently, with mike held low like a broken bottle.* **Boo** *backs off.* **Boo** *signals offstage to someone. Then goes off himself.* **Ray** *turns to audience, dishevelled, some blood on his mouth and nose, sings to some of the lyrics, talks over others.*

Ray (*sings out*) 'Golden days before they end.'

Looking out into audience, hand shielding light.

Ray Bunny Morris. Bunny TV Morris. Where are you? Wherever you are. The bastard drinks are on me.

(*Sings.*) 'Your baby won't be near you any more.' Not tonight, not any night! (*Sings out.*) 'Tender nights before they fly.' Aye mine has. (*Sings.*) 'falling stars that seem to cry.' Aye true that's what they do. Can't hack it.

Ladies and gentlemen, I had a dream. (*Flicks mike lead. Sings.*) 'It's over.'

When I think what might have been. (*Spits.*)
(*Sings.*) 'It breaks my heart in two.'
Finished.
(*Sings.*) 'We're through.'
All through, THROUGH.

(*Sings.*) 'It's over. It's over.'

Suddenly juke box is turned off, record cuts out, he carries on.

(*Sings.*) 'Over, Over, OVER!!'

Stops, puts mike back in stand. Leans head on it. Long long pause. Silence.

Slowly he lifts his head. Slowly he walks off. **Boo** *has reappeared, we watch* **Ray** *go.*

Blackness. The same night. Later.

The living room is burnt out, charred furniture and soot everywhere, things melted and scorched. **Mari** *and* **Sadie** *come* *in silhouetted in door. It's too dark for them to see.* **Mari** *tries light switch. Nothing.*

Sadie I'll get me torch.

She goes.

Mari *strikes a match and sees everything. She gasps. The match goes out. She's still very shaken and slaughtered.* **Sadie** *comes back with a torch. Turns it on.*

Mari Look at the bloody crap of it. Me last home and testament gone up in flames, burnt to buggery. Sadie, I'm gutted. I'm gutted tut' twat bone wi' all this. Look at me ornaments, look at me home. Sadie, Sadie try getting some sugar now, it'll be caramel burnt. I tell you. You might like it, but I wouldn't. I wouldn't.

The phone rings.

Mari I told you about this phone din't I? Din't I? I knew it had some science to it.

She picks up melted phone.

Mari Hello, hell here. (*Listens.*) You got wrong number.

She puts phone down.

Sadie Who were that?

Mari Some official bastard wanting to know if Mari Hoff was still alive. Now then. Oh, Sadie, when I need picking up off the ceiling and the floor, who's left, but you, hey Sade? Hey, who thinks about me, but you. You're a friend, all lard and love, an't you? Come here. (*Hugs her.*) Sadie, your armpits have that smell of cat food again, what have I told you? Wash there.

Sadie Okay.

Mari Okay, rub-a-dub. Bloody hell, at least I'll be able to find you in the dark. Oh, what am I to do, Sade. Let's look up, might not be as bad.

They go upstairs. **Mari** *goes in her bedroom. Screams a little. Comes out.*

Mari All gone. Hopeless. Barbecued bed. Doorless wardrobes full of cinders. Sadie, where did I go wrong? Tipped from one trouble into another all my life. It seems I have to have the flames to feel alive but they always burn. Always burn me. Sadie, what's to become of me now? No house, I lost me job for never going back, no family, no man, where's Mr Ray now? Feeding somewhere else no doubt. Sadie, look at me. My hair piled crinkly on my head like a shock. Affixiated with years of lacquer. My skin creasing and folding faster than I can fill it in. Booze eyes and lashes, my lashes, my fifty lashes. Oh sod it Sade. Sod the whole burnt and choking chunk of my life so far.

She opens the door to **LV**'s *room.*

Mari Well, look at this, would you believe it? Only singed.

Sees records.

Mari Look, look what's not burnt.

She goes over to them.

Mari Look, the seeds of my downfall, the bitter beanstalk beaning circle beginnings that broke Mother's back. They go now.

She lets them fall out of their covers through the open window. They tumble into the alley and smash.

Mari Oh yes, they go now.

She sits on the bed punching the faces on the LP covers.

Mari You and you and you. You tooked my husband, played his heart till it stopped. You took my daughter, my walls. Take that.

She throws them out too, all out of their covers so they smash below.

Mari There, there. Down you go into smithereen alley. Crescendo. Crescendo on that hard gutter floor. I'm coming too.

She climbs onto window sill. **Sadie** *grabs her back. Holds her waist. She flops forward like a rag doll in* **Sadie**'s *arms. Suddenly they hear a van pulling up. They look out the window.*

Mari (*to* **Sadie**) Out with the light. Hide.

They are heard scuttling about in the dark. Then stillness as the door opens and **Billy** *and* **LV** *come in. They stand silhouetted in the doorway.*

Billy I don't think you should be here. It's too dark. Come on away.

LV *just stands.*

Billy I'm not sure you should be.

LV *just stands.*

Billy Come on, let's go. You can get whatever you want tomorrow in the light. Come on, Little Voice.

Billy *turns to go, taking her with him. She stops him pleadingly.*

LV (*almost inaudible*) Please.

Billy I've some lights from work in the van, let me fetch them in.

He goes out. **LV** *stays in the dark.* **Billy** *comes in with the lights. When he puts them down, they illuminate the room, one* *orange, one yellow. They are the self-contained light units used around holes etc. They make the place look like a set for hell in an old theatre melodrama. Their faces are illuminated strangely from below in the orange and yellow lights and massive shadows are thrown up the back.*

Billy Shall I stay with you?

LV No.

Billy I'll wait outside.

LV No.

Billy You can't stay here on your . . . Okay, I'll nip back down the club. I'll finish off, then come back for you. Wait by the corner. Don't stay in here.

LV *doesn't answer. He looks at her. He kisses her gently on the face. He goes.*

LV *turns to stairs and makes her way up. Suddenly, bedroom door bursts open and* **Mari** *comes out.*

Mari What happened, eh? What happened here, then!

LV (*screams*) Aarrgh!

Mari The little match girl who goes burning everything, everything, everything down then.

LV *frantically shakes her head.*

Mari Yes. Yes. My house is a stub. My home a grate.

LV *steps back.* **Mari** *pursues her.*

Mari Now then girl.

Mari *almost grabs her. Suddenly* **Sadie** *sits up from floor.* **LV** *screams again.*

Mari Sadie!

Sadie Sorry.

Sadie *gets up and goes out.*

Mari (*to* **LV**) Where's your burns?

LV *looks scared.*

Mari Exactly. They is none.

LV *backs up.* **Mari** *charges at her.* **LV** *moves.* **Mari** *falls on settee. Mounds of soot fly up into the air, she can't be seen for a second, then the soot descends. She is sitting on the settee facing out. The orange and yellow lights strangely illuminating her face from below, her shadow thrown huge up the back.*

Mari I'm now in the carcass of my house, a smoked ham. I can't start again. What's the next move. I'm too beat for a man, really I ask you. I've been jumping the coals for years, now I've finally fallen in. Nobody wants the burnt bits, have you noticed. They love a blazing bint but when the flames have gone who wants the char? Well, some might say I've got what I deserve. But that's the problem, I've never had what I deserved. I was more than this dump I had to live in. In fact, my energy itself could have burnt this place down years ago, four times over with fireworks forever. I was more than what I married. Your Father, your Father kissing me with his parlour lips. I had health and breasts and legs. I strode. When I got behind your pram I propelled it about a hundred miles an hour. The air was full of the sound of wolf whistles, deafening. He was shambling somewhere behind, a beanpole Chaplin. But you, you were always his. It was always you and him, you and him all the time, doing quiet things, heads bent together, listening to the records. Driving me mad, my energy could have burnt this house down four times over, and you two tilted into books, listening the radio shows, playing board games in front of the fire. Fuck it. And now I'm dancing on my own grave and it's a roasting tin. My house gutted, my last possession gone. My last chance charred. Look at me up to my ankles in char. (*Looking at all the thick soot over the floor*). In fact, this is my soul leaking over the floor here, soot itself. I'm going to scoop handfuls up and spread it over you. Your head, you see, was the match head to this. (*Indicating everything.*)

She gets up with her hands full of soot, and traps **LV** *in a corner. Holding her with one hand while she prepares to cover her with the soot from the other, she holds her there, then . . .*

Mari Wait a minute. No. What do you want anyway? Oh, I know, your records.

She lets her go.

The firemen put all the salvage in the alley. They should be there.

LV *goes out and round to the alley.* **Mari** *stays put.* **LV** *sees the big pile of broken records almost filling the alley. Lamplight glinting off them. She gently picks a piece up. Opens her mouth to scream but nothing comes out. Opens her mouth again, nothing.* **Mari** *appears.*

Mari What's up, cat got your tongue?

Mari *steps forward but she slips on the massive pile of broken records, slithering all over in them and falls.* **LV** *quickly holds the sharp edge of a half record to her throat.* **Mari** *suddenly stunned.*

LV And now, you will listen! One time, one! (**LV** *screams.*) There's one. (*Screams again.*) There's another. Can you hear me now my Mother! (*Words rush out.*) My Dad, you mention him and it's wrong what you say, wrong what you say. You drove him as fast as you could to an early grave. With your men and your shouting and your pals and your nights, your nights, your nights, your nights, your nights of neglect. Things forgotten everywhere. No soap in the dish, no roll in the toilet, no clean blouse for school. Oh my Dad, when he had his records on he sparkled, not dazzling like you, but with fine lights, fine lights! He couldn't speak up to you, cause he must have wanted you so. I couldn't speak up to you, cause I could never get a word in! (*Looks at piece of record in her hand.*) These become my tongues. (*Drops it.*) And now they've gone, I don't know where this is coming from. But it's one after another and I can tell you now.

Pause.

That you hurt me.

Pause.

That you hurt me.

Pause.

With your sharp ways and the things you said and your SELFISHNESS WOMAN!

Pause.

I've got to stop now. I'm trembling so strange.

She drifts slowly away. **Mari** *on her knees, trying to stand. Pleading.*

Mari LV, I beseech you. I beseech you, LV.

Mari *is slipping, trying to stand but slipping in all the records. Soot all over her hands and face, in the lamplight, slipping, sliding, trying to stand.*

Mari I beseech you! I beseech you!

She stops struggling, flops face down in the pile.

Mari Slithered at last into the dirt gut of the twat of life, upended in an alley. I knew in my true heart there were nothing else for it, no matter how hard I tried I could not avoid what fate had reserved for me all along, the famous 'Tart's end', an old girl left dirty on her belly in an alley, homeless and juiceless and tootless and solid stone cold alone.

She closes her eyes. **Sadie** *is at alley end, peeping and softly giggling.*

Blackout.

Lights come up on the empty club. **LV** *comes in, stands at back of stage. Suddenly, faint purring sound of machinery.* **LV** *looks up.* **Billy** *comes into view in 'Cherry Picker'.*

Billy You come back on your own. I was just coming. Everything alright?

She nods.

I've just to fit this last un, then it's done.

He goes back up. We can't see him. **LV** *just standing, staring up at him, then all around, and at the stage where she suffered. He comes back down into view, this time continuing right to stage. Gets out.*

You sure you alright?

She nods.

You want to see display now?

She nods. He has installed his own expensive and amazing lights and effects into the club rig and all around. He operates them from a hand-held remote control.

Right. First a few lights.

He presses control, lights come on beautifully, spraying colours, then soaking the stage in deep blue.

And music.

He presses control. Powerful orchestral arrangement of Judy Garland song comes on. He changes lights again, again, through the building introduction, an incredible display. She is awestruck at it all, dizzied by it.

Sing if you feel like it.

She looks at him.

Sing Little Voice. Go on.

The lights suddenly become so powerful that they seem to lift her in the air, the music too. She closes her eyes, starts to sing, quiet at first, she opens her eyes to see millions of tiny white lights sprayed all over the stage. She sings louder holding up her hands like catching snow or stars.

Go on, louder.

He changes the lights again. She sings out.

Sing for yourself.

She sings out, stepping forward, louder, clearer as the lights beat and flash higher and higher weaving breathtaking patterns.

You're singing in your own voice. Your own.

She's singing full, confident, loud, tears coming down her face. She moves as she sings now. She's near the 'Cherry Picker'.

Get in. Go on. Go on.

She does. **Billy** *operates the 'Picker' it begins to ascend as she sings. Sings. The 'Picker' rising higher and higher. He changes to lasers, beautiful beams, breathtaking patterns across the space. She rises into them higher and higher, up in the lights, singing, singing, singing in her own voice.*

The End.

Production Notes

Music

All songs throughout the play should be suited to the actress playing LV and the production:
The unaccompanied song, page 16.
The two performances, page 44 and 58.
The breakdown scene (sung and spoken), page 72.
The final song, page 85.

Although the choice of artists should remain in keeping with the type of Diva and singer LV's father would listen to, even a little opera may be appropriate.

Bearing the above in mind, any other music used in the play can be a matter of choice.

The first act in the club (page 44) can have simple accompaniment, (i.e. organ and drums) or be sung unaccompanied, or a combination of these, i.e. the first two songs accompanied and the last unaccompanied.

The second club act (page 58) should have an excellent backing, live or recorded, or a combination of both.

The organ and drums, and drums alone, may be used for music between scenes, if required.

Cuts and alterations to the text

In some subsequent productions, the following cuts and alterations were made:

Page 4, cut as follows:

Mari . . . or should I say Clark Gable.

She laughs.

Hurry up lads.

Page 6, cut Aunty Slit phone-call as follows:

. . . last glance upstairs, leaves. **Mari** *begins dialling.* **LV**
enters down the stairs. Picks up newspaper. Heads for kitchen.

LV I hope you've paid for that.

Mari Oh shut up, it's me new toy and in fact . . .

Continues as written. If this cut is made, alter the
following line on page 8:

Mari *sits on sofa.*

Mari Come on cock, make us a cuppa.

Page 9, cut as follows:

Mari . . . You emptied half the bloody bag yesterday.
Do you like me phone?

Page 10, cut as follows:

Mari (*to* **LV**) Did you hear that. (*To* **Sadie**.) Bloody
crazed chil' she is. She bugs me at times. Though
I'm . . .

Mari . . . records her Dad left her, over and a over, on
and on. That's not . . . . .

Page 10/11, the following, cut sequence, may be used.

Mari Go on, drink it now.

They both drink.

Mari Well, Sadie, what a night! What-a-night! What a
championship neet! I copped off again with that Ray. I
did it again! He had no choice Sadie. The club turn
was a romantic singer, thank frig, and the music was in
our heads, in our heads, and in his wandering hands.
He knows so many people – 'Howdo Ray' 'Alright Ray'.
You can see how I am there. Queen. Queen for the
night. He motored me home about a million miles an
hour, then screeching to a halt outside, did you not
hear us? You must be dead if you didn't. I saw every
other curtain in the bitching road twitch. Then he
comes at me with this pronto snog, lip-lapping like hell.

That's men for you in it Sade, if you can remember.
Lip-a-lapping like old hell he was. But at least he's a lot
better than most, at least he knows how to slide and
dart and take a throat. At least there's always the thick
wad of his wallet up against your tit for comfort.

Sadie Aye.

Mari And he's got a finger in so many pies, Sadie.
Some too hot for his own good if you get my meaning.
In fact, he's moving into artist's management at the
moment, you know. Yes. He's got a crooner, a dog act
and two strippers at the moment. But he'll make it,
he'll make it in anything, Ray Say. See, that's why I got
the (*indicating phone*) ragbone in. I've got to be on call.
It's got to be smooth for him going out with me. I must
win him. I've got to keep him. He's got a lot of young
bitches into him a quart my age. I know they haven't
got my wizzle and mince but I'm taking no chances
Sade, how can I at my time of strife?

Page 14.

The film can be any film featuring one of the artists,
i.e. Gracie Fields.

Page 15.

The direction concerning the bottles may be shortened
to an action, where she goes to one place and gathers
up an armful of bottles, too many to hold properly, and
places them down on the coffee table. Backs off.

Mari There.

Page 17:

Mari's record should be someone like Tom Jones or
Barry Manilow or Julio Iglesias.

Page 17:
LV's singing must be orchestrated in with the dialogue
happening below so that Ray and Mari can be heard.
For example:

Mari . . . that's not the record, that's LV.
(**LV** *has faded her singing down to a low hum.*)

Scene continues to page 18:

Mari . . . could not succeed.

(*Song returns now, building up to volume.*)

Come on lover boy.

Ray (*still towards the singing*) Hang on, I'm listening.

Page 21:
The impersonation can be altered to anyone the actress
can do well. For example:

Ray . . . And of course Lulu.

LV Lulu?

Ray Yeah.

Continue as written until:

. . . *while he's distracted and not looking, she sings at full blast
the opening wail from 'Shout' by Lulu.* **Ray** *turns white.*

(Incidentally, the distraction direction given of the
wallet, can be anything that diverts him for a second –
cigarette, etc.).

Page 37: In some productions the whole of the last
scene of the first act (pages 37–42) has been cut
altogether. Act One then ends with LV singing
'Somewhere over the Rainbow'.

Page 44: When the lights go out, it may be better to avoid total darkness so that the audience can just make LV out and see that she is singing.

Page 46: If the actor playing Billy is small, the following alternative may be used:

Mari Clear off. Go on. Shrimp on heat. Piss it. Go.

Page 54: The effect of LV in the long glittering dress may be saved until later in the scene. If this is decided upon, then the scene should open with Mari rushing downstairs calling for Sadie. When Sadie appears, she comes running downstairs from bathroom or Mari's bedroom, as though she has been in there helping LV. LV then makes her first appearance in the scene when Sadie brings her down (page 57).

Pages 58/59: A cage effect can be used for the beginning of the second club act, for example:

Ray *brings on a blindfolded* **LV**. *Lights illuminate a big cut-out cage. He leads her behind it, turns her upstage, back to the audience, removes the blindfold. He steps away. Signals for the music to begin. Exits. Orchestration of 'Goldfinger' begins. The cage ascends.* **LV** *slowly turns around . . .*

Page 65/66: Cut the phone call, as follows:

She sadly puts them on the table by her and leaves. She goes back downstairs.

Mari She won't touch 'em, Sadie. She's not . . .

If the phone call has been cut, make the following addition to the speech on page 66:

. . . I wonder if we're not pushing her too hard, you know. Four, five spots at the club already. One show after another . . .

Page 75:

If the production is using a revolve stage for the burnt out house, then the last scene in the club may be cut altogether if preferred – from LV in the burning house (p.75) to the burnt out house (p.76). The following is another version of the last club scene without juke box accompaniment:

The club is packed. **Mr Boo** *excited and worried. Sweat pouring off him. Caught in mid-speech:*

Mr Boo She'll be here any minute I assure you all. I never thought we could get so many in. What a star turn eh! She'll be here soon. She will.

Loud scuffle and fight offstage.

(*Off mike.*) What the . . .

Looking off stage.

Ray! (*To audience.*) Ray Say's here.

(*Off, to musicians.*) Play the introduction. Play the introduction.

LV's *introduction music starts up.*

Here she is Ladies and Gentlemen. What you've all been waiting for, the . . .

Ray *appears onstage.* **Boo** *still presenting, turns, is shocked to see* **Ray** *on stage.* **Ray** *grabs mike without looking at* **Boo.** *He is drunk, manic, blood round his mouth.*

Mr Boo (*angry, trying to get his mike back*) Hey!

Ray *bundles him in corner, head-butts him.* **Boo** *screams out in pain. The intro music stops, discordant.*

Mr Boo (*holding his face*) Bastard. Bastard. (*Going off.*) You're finished!

Ray faces audience. Stares out.
Starts to sing, unaccompanied 'It's Over' by Ray Orbison. After a few lines stops.

Then, looking out into audience, hand shielding the light.

Ray Bunny Morris. Bunny T.V. Morris. Where are you? Wherever you are, the bastard drinks are on me.

Continues with the song until he reaches:

Over, Over, OVER!!'

Stops, lets his head drop on mike stand. Long, long pause. Silence. Turns, walks slowly away.

Page 84:
Cut Mari's last speech, so that stage directions run on:

She stops struggling, flops face down in the pile. She closes her eyes. . . .

Page 84, final scene:
LV can approach the stage through the auditorium if preferred.

Page 84:
If preferred LV can be on stage alone in the last scene. Billy can leave the stage as follows:

Billy You want see display now?

She nods. He goes off through theatre.

He calls out the rest of his lines to her as if in lighting box.

Page 84:
If the Cherry Picker cannot be brought onto the stage for the end, an ordinary, straight up and down lighting lift can be used.

Lightning Source UK Ltd.
Milton Keynes UK
11 July 2010

156822UK00001B/44/P